# 715

## REFLECTIONS ON HAMMERIN' HANK & THE HOME RUN THAT MADE HISTORY

### KEVIN NEARY   FOREWORD BY MONTE IRVIN

SPORTS PUBLISHING

Sports Publishing books may be purchased in bulk at special discounts for sales promotion, corporate gifts, fund-raising, or educational purposes. Special editions can also be created to specifications. For details, contact the Special Sales Department, Sports Publishing, 307 West 36th Street, 11th Floor, New York, NY 10018 or sportspubbooks@skyhorsepublishing.com.

Sports Publishing® is a registered trademark of Skyhorse Publishing, Inc.®, a Delaware corporation.

Visit our website at www.sportspubbooks.com.

10 9 8 7 6 5 4 3 2 1

Library of Congress Cataloging-in-Publication Data is available on file.

Cover design by Owen Corrigan
Cover photo credit: Courtesy Atlanta Braves Archives

ISBN: 978-1-61321-763-4
Ebook ISBN: 978-1-61321-786-3

Printed in China

# *Contents*

# *Dedication*

This book is dedicated to my own starting lineup—my three children, Matthew, Emma, and Grace, for their kindness and devotion; and to my wife Sue for her endless support and encouragement.

Hank Aaron, by Ross R. Rossin. 2010. Oil on Canvas. National Portrait Gallery, Smithsonian Institution; gift of Delta Airlines, Inc.

# Acknowledgements

Cindi Adler (Los Angeles Dodgers), Mario Alioto (San Francisco Giants), Jennifer Ardis, Steven Arocho (Major League Baseball), Dave Arrigo (Pittsburgh Pirates), Susan Bailey (Atlanta Braves), Louis Barricelli (MLB Network), Brian Bartow (St. Louis Cardinals), Benjamin Baughman, Bethany Bentley (Smithsonian Institute), Court Berry-Tripp (Cleveland Indians), Matthew Birch (California Angels of Anaheim), John Blake (Texas Rangers), John Boggs, Jack Bonnikson, Greg Bouris (Major League Baseball Players Association), Steve Brener, Brain Britten (Detroit Tigers), Adam Buck, Jared Burleyson (Atlanta Braves), Mary Burns (Milwaukee Brewers), Rob Butcher (Cincinnati Reds), Steven Carney (WDAE Host/Anchor), Jason Carr (Chicago Cubs), Elle Carriere (Florentine Films), Matt Chisholm (San Francisco Giants), Adam Chodzko (California Angels of Anaheim), Bonnie Clark (Philadelphia Phillies), Sherry Clawson, Deanna Congileo (The Carter Center), Pat Courtney (Major League Baseball), Chad Crunk (Detroit Tigers), Colby Curry (Kansas City Royals), Allison Davis (Jackie Robinson Foundation), Gene Dias (Houston Astros), Ginger Dillon (Major League Baseball), Dr. Ray Doswell (Negro Leagues Baseball Museum), Chris Eckes (Cincinnati Reds), Patricia McCabe Estrada, Lorraine Fisher (MLB Network), Sean Forman (Sports-Reference.com), Thomas Galton (William J. Clinton Presidential Library), Julie Ganz (Skyhorse Publishing), Trevor Gooby (Pittsburgh Pirates), Denise Gorman, Jonathan Grasseo, Heather Greenberg (The Topps Company), Dave Haller (Tampa Bay Rays),

Dan Hart (Pittsburgh Pirates), Brace Hemmelgarn (Minnesota Twins), Mitch Hestad (Minnesota Twins), Tim Hevly (Seattle Mariners), Andrew Heydt (Minnesota Twins), Diane Hock, Dani Holmes-Kirk (Chicago Cubs), David Holtzman (Kansas City Royals), Quinn Hood, Brad Horn (National Baseball Hall of Fame & Museum), John Horne (National Baseball Hall of Fame & Museum), Jay Horwitz (New York Mets), Jeff Idelson (National Baseball Hall of Fame & Museum), Chris Idol, Josh Ishoo (San Diego Padres), Nate Janoso (Cleveland Indians), Jim Johnson (Detroit Tigers), Angela Jun (The Topps Company), Doug Kemp (Philadelphia Phillies), Pam Kenn (Boston Red Sox), Brittany Kennedy (Minnesota Twins), Mike Kennedy (Minnesota Twins), Paul Kuo (Beverly Hills Sports Council), Patrick Kurish (San Diego Padres), Jerry Lewis (Detroit Tigers), Donny Lowe (National Baseball Hall of Fame & Museum), Jeff Luhnow (Houston Astros), John Maroon, Gori Matsumoto (Fukuoka SoftBank Hawks), Stephanie Mayfield, Stephen Miller, Warren Miller (San Diego Padres), Jim Misudek (Atlanta Braves), Hal Morningstar, Dustin Morse (Minnesota Twins), Craig Muder (National Baseball Hall of Fame & Museum), Kelly Nash (Fox Sports Florida/Sun Sports), Polly Nodine (Jimmy Carter Presidential Library), Patrick O'Connell (Arizona Diamondbacks), Veronica Owens, Paul Pflug, Bret Picciolo (San Diego Padres), Dena Propis (Houston Astros), Herbert Ragan (William J. Clinton Presidential Library), Rich Rice (Texas Rangers), Sheri Rosenberg (Boston Red Sox), Joe Roti (Chicago White Sox), Marty Sewell (Miami Marlins), Larry Shenk (Philadelphia Phillies), Deborah Sisum (Smithsonian Institute), Steven Skelly (Jackie Robinson Foundation), Mireille Stephen, Geoffrey Stone, Amy Summers (Los Angeles Dodgers), Bart Swain (Cleveland Indians), Jody Tabek, Allan Tanenbaum, Garrett Thomas (Los Angeles Dodgers), Jason Thaler (The Topps Company), Frank Thoma, Peggy Thompson (Detroit

Tigers), Rick Thompson (Detroit Tigers), John Timberlake (Philadelphia Phillies), Anne Torres, MJ Trahan (Houston Astros), Jim Trdinich (Pittsburgh Pirates), Craig Vanderkam (Tampa Bay Rays), Mike Vassallo (Milwaukee Brewers), Rick Vaughn (Tampa Bay Rays), Brian Warecki (Pittsburgh Pirates), Harlan Werner, Casey Wilcox (Arizona Diamondbacks), Bev Wilson (The Topps Company), Shana Wilson (San Diego Padres), and Melody Yount (St. Louis Cardinals).

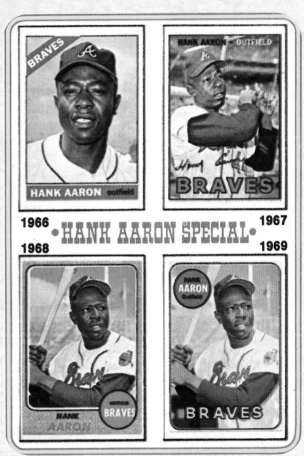

1958 •HANK AARON SPECIAL• 1959    1954 •HANK AARON SPECIAL• 1955

1960 1961    1956 1957

1962 •HANK AARON SPECIAL• 1963

1964 1965

# Foreword

I was a Special Representative for the Commissioner of Baseball under Bowie Kuhn beginning in 1968. My job was to promote baseball all over the world, and in that capacity I was there to witness Hank Aaron hit his record-breaking home run on April 8, 1974.

But I am getting ahead of myself. To understand that moment you have to understand the journey and struggle many of us took in order to get to that day. I was born in Haleburg, Alabama, in the year 1919, and when I turned eight years old the family moved us all to Orange, New Jersey. So, I was raised in New Jersey and that is where I attended school for the first time, and because I was already eight years old they placed me in third grade. Eventually, I went to high school and then to college at Lincoln University, which was right outside of Philadelphia. I enjoyed many sports—track, football, basketball—but baseball was king back then. All of the kids back when I was grow-ing up played baseball. It was *the* sport. It was played in grade school, in middle school, in high school, and in college. Wherever you saw a sandlot or playground there were generally kids playing baseball, no matter what time of day it was. We played baseball from the morning to the night. Again, baseball was king and yet even though I loved this game so much I knew that I couldn't do it for a living. There wasn't the money there is today. And all we could aspire to was the Negro

Leagues back then. There wasn't a Jackie Robinson yet who would go on and change everything for the better for so many of us. But after Jackie did come around and break the color barrier so many of us then had aspirations of going higher. We weren't envious of Jackie, but some of us

were jealous because we wondered why Jackie was chosen to be the first. I was fortunate to play alongside with some of the greats of the Negro Leagues. Players like Josh Gibson, who they called the "Babe Ruth of the Negro Leagues," Cool Papa Bell, Willie Wells, Satchel Paige, Buck Leonard, and Oscar Charleston, who many would say was the greatest ever. Charleston could do it all; he could run, field, throw, and hit for tremendous power. I was very close with Josh Gibson. The two of us became great friends and we spent a lot of happy moments just talking about baseball. I remember pitchers during my day would say, almost in a bragging sense, "Did you see the home run that Josh Gibson hit off of me last night?" And then there was the team Gibson

Courtesy of the National Baseball Hall of Fame and Museum

played on, it was the Kansas City Monarchs; they were called the New York Yankees of the Negro Leagues. They had some tremendous teams. They were a powerhouse. The Monarchs could hit and pitch so well. Remarkably, most of these players still only earned about $200 a month and the average player earned about $100 a month. But we played because we loved the game so much. I remember we got a dollar a day, which was called field money. Back then a dollar could get you two good meals a day, some dessert, and if the waitress was pretty you even had a nickel or a dime for her tip! Again, the money wasn't there, but no one seemed to care. We were young and we were playing the game we loved.

At times, we'd play a Sunday doubleheader in Newark, and the next day we'd be back at it again, this time in Washington, DC. It was crazy. We'd never complain because of the passion we had for the game. I remember we got better at sleeping on the bus than in hotels. Depending on the city we played in there were obstacles we all had to overcome. There were some diners, restaurants, and hotels at which we were not welcomed. But there were also a collection of these establishments which were owned by African Americans who did welcome us. I always felt sorry for many of these businesses because when Jackie Robinson broke the color barrier these businesses suffered because many of the black ballplayers started to frequent these locations that they were once restricted from entering. Yet, that was the way things were back then. Things changed when Jackie broke the color barrier, and eventually the Negro Leagues suffered because of the influx of black players into the major leagues and they soon went out of business. With progress there has to be change. I remember I was angry, and many others were as well, that we were not permitted to enter these locations, but for me I never understood their anger. I could never understand how one human being could have so much anger towards another human being just because of the color of their skin. Even in my own neighborhood of Orange, New Jersey, I wasn't allowed to frequent some locations. I remember on the day I graduated high school there was a restaurant two blocks from the school; many of my fellow classmates went to celebrate, but it was off-limits to blacks. You go to school and learn about the land of the free and the home of the brave and for so many of us that wasn't the case. Many of my friends, who were white, didn't understand it either. The funny thing about segregation in baseball was that those fans who truly loved the game never got the chance to see some of the greatest ballplayers that ever played this game because they played in the Negro Leagues. I often refer to this as the biggest crime that has ever occurred in the game, that someone like a Babe Ruth never got the chance to face off against the likes of Satchel Paige or that Walter Johnson never had the opportunity to pitch against Josh Gibson. I remember Walter Johnson said to a reporter one day that "someone ought to give a player like Josh Gibson a chance." Even Babe Ruth once said something similar, but you never hear about those stories. Then there was Dizzy Dean, who was quoted as saying that he wished Satchel Paige and he would have played on the same St. Louis team. He said to Satchel, "You and I could be going fishing together in July if we were teammates." There were other major league ballplayers who asked the same question too because they were such fierce competitors and they were the ones who were always looking to compete against the best.

It's funny, there was no such thing as segregation on the ball field until you became a professional. When you were a kid playing in the sandlots nobody cared about color, primarily because when you are a kid you don't see color. It's only when you get older that you see the differences. I remember when Jackie did break into the game he did give us hope, but it was still an experiment, which most people didn't realize. I called it the Jackie Robinson experiment because if he failed, the door of opportunity would have slammed shut for us for years to come. But he was a success, and the rest is history.

Over the years, many people ask me what was the highlight of my career? The highlight of my career was in 1951 when Bobby Thomson hit the home run that was heard around the world . . . And in 1973, when I was inducted in the National Baseball Hall of Fame, that was a pretty special moment for me as well. Any time you are honored by your peers is a special moment and thrill and it made for a special day that I will always appreciate and will always remember. I still think about that day fondly even today.

Henry "Hank" Aaron was just a teenage boy from Mobile, Alabama when Jackie Robinson helped change the world by opening a door that Hank Aaron would pass through one day. Interestingly, if you take the number 47, the year Jackie Robinson broke the color barrier, and reverse it you get 74, just like the year 1974 when on another April day, Henry Aaron surpassed Babe Ruth to become the greatest home run hitter of all time.

—Monte Irvin (National Baseball Hall of Fame, class of 1973)

# Introduction

For all of us, there are certain moments in the course of human history we remember so vividly. They normally involve personal milestones in our lives or they pertain to a subject that is near and dear to our understanding. We remember where we were and what we were doing during those moments. For me, it was April 8, 1974, I was nine years old, and it still feels like it was yesterday. I was sitting next to my father on the sofa watching Hank Aaron prepare to eclipse the all-time home run mark set by the legendary Babe Ruth. At the time, hitting 714 home runs was considered somewhat of a magical and unsurpassable feat. Yet, through determination, consistency, and commitment Hank Aaron went on to break the record and become the undisputed Home Run King.

I remember I was in my first year of Little League then and I was entering the sport with a pretty good knowledge of the game, thanks to my father, who taught me all too well the stories of the ball players he considered the greatest of all time. These names included Aaron, Ted Williams, Willie Mays, Al Kaline, Stan Musial, Joe DiMaggio, and Mickey Mantle, just to name a few. At the time, my great-uncle was also living with us and he too was a huge baseball fan. Being significantly older than my father, my great-uncle could talk at length about the greatest players from his day, such as Babe Ruth, Walter Johnson, Honus Wagner, Carl Hubbell, Jimmie Foxx, Lou Gehrig, Ty Cobb, and Cy Young. Certainly, this education was not just exclusive to my family, but that is what makes baseball so unique. There is a popular expression that goes like this, "History begins the year that you are born," but when it comes to the typical baseball family, history has no specified barrier. You see time differently when you follow baseball. Baseball continues to embrace its history like no other sport; it honors its past while it connects the various generations.

I always believed Hank Aaron would be a fascinating subject for any book because of how he was able to connect several significant timeframes for baseball. He was one of the last players to play in the major leagues who came over from the Negro Leagues. In addition, he had some uncanny resemblances with the ever-popular Babe Ruth. Like Ruth, Aaron was also born in February, (Ruth on the 6th and Aaron on the 5th); they both hit their 714th home runs while in a Braves uniform; and they were both forty years old when they achieved this milestone.

Yet despite my fascination with Hank Aaron's career, as I began writing this book I quickly realized what little I actually knew about Hank the man. As a fan and a student of the game, I could recite statistics regarding his career, like the number of hits he had, or RBI, or which teams he played for. But as the book developed, what became obvious was that Hank Aaron was much more than an acclaimed home run hitter.

As the book evolved, it became more of a tribute book and a time capsule of this incredible man and the people he touched along the way. I felt as though I was an observer through time as I was constructing this elaborate puzzle concerning Hank Aaron. The subject became a recipe for success because of all of the individuals who wanted to step up and speak about what Hank Aaron meant to them. And, it didn't just involve those from the baseball world. People from all over, from the political arena to entertainment, had something to say about the greatness of this man and what he has meant not only to the game of baseball but to society in general.

Despite the array of people highlighted in this book, the section I enjoyed working on the most involved the current players of today. Not one of them was even alive when Hank Aaron played the game. They weren't even a twinkle in their mother's eye at the time. They were only exposed to Hank Aaron through the magic of videos and highlight reels. And yet, in each of their cases, they spoke very passionately about him and how they had this iconic vision of Hank Aaron and what impact he has had on their game and their lives.

But my favorite quote about Aaron that I came across during my research came from a legendary baseball pitcher, Curt Simmons, who said, "Throwing a fastball by Hank Aaron is like trying to sneak the sunrise past a rooster." I couldn't have said it better myself, Curt.

After I'd compiled the interviews for the body of the book, I then went back and teamed up with the legendary Monte Irvin to write the book's foreword. Mr. Irvin has been a witness to history in his

90-plus years. Like Aaron, he too made the transition from the Negro Leagues to the major leagues. He too was inducted into the National Baseball Hall of Fame and he was there representing the Commissioner of Baseball and his office when Hank Aaron hit his record-breaking home run in 1974. It was an honor to be able to work with Monte Irvin on this and to hear his thoughts firsthand.

My only hope as an author is that you enjoy this book as much as I did putting it all together.

—Kevin Neary

# Honor Roll

"April 8, 1974 was a great day for baseball and for America as we watched Hank Aaron round the bases for a record-breaking 715th time.

"Hank's ability to pile up home runs was about much more than just his skills. What made Hank a once-in-a-lifetime hitter was his consistency, which was rooted in his focus, his humility, and his

respect for the game. He showed up every day and never allowed himself to get too high or too low; he wouldn't let a hot streak lull him into complacency, and he knew the end of a slump was always just one swing away. That's how he became the only player in history to hit 30 or more home runs in 15 seasons, and why, from the time I was in elementary school until after I had finished law school, Hank's success at bat just seemed to be one of life's natural rhythms: every spring the trees blossom, and Hank Aaron begins wearing out the pitchers of the National League.

"What's most impressive about Hank's inner strength and mental fortitude is that he could concentrate on every at-bat in a time of continuing discrimination. People often forget that he broke into the big leagues just a few years after Jackie Robinson, and faced many of the same indignities throughout his career. The fact that he was able to overcome such obstacles—and especially the hateful fever pitch that surrounded his approach of Babe Ruth's record—is an extraordinary testament to his character.

"My life has been blessed by the friendship of Hank and his wife Billye, who also deserves some credit for the way he kept his eye on the ball. On the weekend before the election in 1992, Hank appeared with me at a rally in Atlanta. There were 25,000 people there. Three days later, I carried Georgia by 13,000 votes. He's never let me forget who made me President!

"Now I've known Hank and Billye for more than two decades. His service to others in those years is as remarkable as his baseball career. He is a relentless advocate for civil rights, and through his Chasing the Dream Foundation, he's giving underprivileged young people opportunities to thrive. Hank's life and career have been great gifts to America, and the best way we can try to repay him is by following his inspiring example and working toward a brighter future for all."

—President William Jefferson Clinton (42nd President of the United States)

3

"I was thrilled to witness Hank Aaron's record-breaking 715th home run on April 8, 1974. Having integrated sports in the Deep South, Aaron already was a hero to me as I sat in the stands that day. As the first black superstar playing on the first big league baseball team in the Deep South, he had been both demeaned and idolized in Atlanta.

"It was obvious that he was not completely comfortable with the fanfare that greeted him before that eventful game. A humble man who did not seek limelight, he just wanted to play baseball, which he did exquisitely.

"I always have shared the opinion of other southern political leaders that Hank Aaron's place in the evolution of the civil rights movement never was properly regarded. Having sports teams legitimized us and gave us the opportunity to be known for something that was not going to be a national embarrassment, and Aaron was no small part of that. He became the first black man for whom white fans in the South cheered."

—President Jimmy Carter (39th President of the United States)

"Hank Aaron's 715th career home run remains one of the most indelible moments in baseball history. I always admired Hank not just for the way he played, but also for the way he carried himself—particularly the courage with which he earned the most distinguished record in American sports. Hank always let his deeds do the talking for him.

"My fondest memory as a fan was when I saw Hank's pennant-clinching, 11th inning homer against the Cardinals on September 23, 1957 from the stands at County Stadium. When Hank passed Babe Ruth on the all-time home run list on April 8, 1974 in Atlanta, the feat marked the culmination of a career of all-around excellence, consistency, and quiet dignity. It was a privilege to witness the height of his career in Milwaukee, and bringing him back to my hometown as a Brewer to conclude his career will always rank among the personal highlights of my three decades with the franchise.

"Most importantly, Hank has long been one of my dearest and most loyal friends, and he has never changed. The work ethic and approach that took him to the top of the all-time home run list for 33 years are exemplary for all those in baseball and beyond.

"Hank Aaron has led an extraordinary American life, which transcends his many achievements on the diamond. The national pastime is fortunate that a human being like him will stand among the pillars of the game forever."

—Commissioner of Major League Baseball Allan H. (Bud) Selig

"Hank Aaron has led an extraordinary American life, which transcends his many achievements on the diamond. The national pastime is fortunate that a human being like him will stand among the pillars of the game forever."

—Commissioner Bud Selig

Courtesy of Major League Baseball

"From a personal standpoint, there is no one I feel closer to in this game or that I respect more than Hank Aaron. I've known him since 1962, when I led a small group of investors to buy the Milwaukee Braves. I enjoy being around Hank as much as I can and he continues to be the face of our franchise here in Atlanta. But then again, he has always had that role, since his playing days. Hank was such a tremendous talent. In my opinion, there are so many things that he did well and he was never recognized to the point he should have. For example, I never saw him miss a cutoff man or make a mistake on the bases. Hank could do it all. Hank was also such a smart ballplayer. I can never say enough about how great he was. Hank has always been quietly underestimated by those in baseball, but not by me or by anyone in the Atlanta Braves organization. I'll tell you, Hank was absolutely the greatest ballplayer that has ever played this game, according to my book. And, off the field he has created a wonderful life for himself and for so many others. For example, Hank's Chasing the Dream Foundation has helped so many and it continues to do some extraordinary things. Hank has truly touched so many.

"I remember the two of us, Hank and I, were recently in attendance during the official ground-breaking for the Atlanta Braves' new stadium. The governor of Georgia was there and about 300 to 400 other invited guests and media were on hand. Many got up and spoke and as each one got up there was modest applause, but then when Hank got up to speak he brought the house down. Hank spoke so beautifully, but then again that is what he is able to do each time the moment presents itself. Hank is so loved and it was an honor for me recently to be on hand and speak when they honored him in February, 2014 at the Smithsonian Institute during his 80th birthday celebration. But again, it just never seemed that Hank ever got the credit he should have received.

Courtesy of the Atlanta Braves

"Take, for example, during the 1980s Hank was our Farm Director responsible for bringing up new talent to the ball club. In theory, the work that Hank did then helped get things started and going, so when the 1990s came around we had the talent to go out there and win 14 straight titles.

"I especially love being with Hank during each Spring Training and walking around with him on the field and in the clubhouse. So many of the young players want to seek him out and talk with him. Hank talks to them all and he gives them so much of his time. Hank is just this terrific guy . . . I can't say enough. Hank has also been such a positive influence on the city of Atlanta. He still calls the city his home. He remains very active in the community. Hank's even on the Board of Directors for the Atlanta Falcons. Wherever he goes people are just excited to see him and during the whole march to the record back in 1974 he handled himself so well.

"I remember the day he broke Babe Ruth's record and I had the privilege of looking after his mother and father, who were in my box that day near the dugout. I remember thinking about the celebration we were hoping to have and how it was going to be handled and fortunately Hank accommodated us by hitting that home run. When it was first hit I wasn't sure that he got enough of it, but he did. It was a classic Hank Aaron swing. As soon as we knew it was gone I started to help his mother and father get to home plate to be there with their son. It was a tender and emotional moment. It was such a great day and a great moment for America. This was a story all Americans could love and be proud of."

—William C. Bartholomay (Former owner Milwaukee/Atlanta Braves)

Courtesy of the Atlanta Braves

"I've known Mr. Aaron for forty years, having met him first in November 1974. I met Mr. Aaron in person for the first time at the official press conference for the Home Run Derby between the Home Run King of the United States and Japan, which was held at Tokyo's Korakuen Stadium in front of 50,000 fans to determine who was the greatest Home Run hitter in the world. I was so surprised and shocked about the size of Mr. Aaron's hands and hips. His body frame was so big and the gap of the body size between the two of us was just like the heavyweight boxer versus the flyweight boxer. However, my first impression of Mr. Aaron through the conversations we had was that he was very calm and he was a real gentleman. After the competition, we didn't talk to each other much during our playing years, but after we both went into retirement, we had a great time every time when we reunited and we enjoyed sharing our passion about the game we love. My best memory of Mr. Aaron was when I was invited to his home in a suburb of Atlanta during the Japan All-Star vs Major League Baseball All-Star Games.  I was so overwhelmed by the size of the gate to enter his property. I was also surprised by the distance between the entry gate and his home. I could not believe how large Mr. Aaron's home was. My first thought was that I better not invite him to my home because it was not nearly the same size.  I remember he had a tennis court on his property and he told me that it was a gift from the Atlanta Braves because the Braves knew that he trained his legs by playing tennis in the offseason.  Other than the tennis court, he had a very large pond that took up half of his land and had many large-mouth bass in the pond. In fact, Mr. Aaron had a big trophy bass hanging on his wall that he caught in that pond.

"My favorite story involving Mr. Aaron would have to be about the World Children's Baseball Fair. After my retirement, I shot a coffee commercial with Mr. Aaron in 1990. The coffee was called J.O. I remember shooting the commercial and during our breaks we would share our passion for the game of baseball. During our conversations we came to the conclusion that we needed to share this passion with the rest of the world. We concluded that we must help to develop baseball all over the world. From this conclusion, the World Children's Baseball Fair was established and held in Los Angeles in 1990. We had our 24th annual fair this past season! In my opinion, I don't think someone like Mr. Aaron—who is not only the Major League Baseball all-time Home Run King, but has 23 years of major league service with the historical record of 3,771 total career hits, which is just after the legendary greatest hitter, Mr. Ty Cobb, and he was also well known as a great defender—would come to Japan. But if Mr. Aaron did come to Japan, he would be my best teammate without any doubts, but I also wanted to make myself capable to compete well for the Home Run King as a rival to him, rather than being just a best teammate to him."

—Sadaharu Oh (Retired Japanese–Taiwanese baseball player and manager who holds the world lifetime home run record, having hit 868 home runs during his professional career. Referred to as the "Babe Ruth of Japan.")

"While Hank Aaron will forever be remembered as the man who broke the sport's greatest record, hitting his 715th homer, I will always cherish our friendship and remember him as a man who symbolizes excellence, commitments, and grace."

—Rachel Robinson (Wife of Baseball great Jackie Robinson)

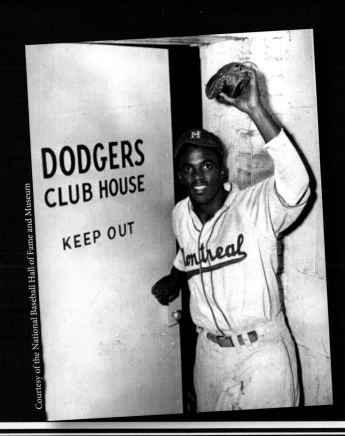

Courtesy of the National Baseball Hall of Fame and Museum

"I know and love him well. It is a great honor to know him. Hank is like a father figure to me. My father would often speak about one's strength of character and to be consistent and I feel that same relationship with Hank Aaron. He has always been a warm, generous, and loving man. He is wonderfully committed to his wife, his family, and his friends. He also has this wonderful bond with young people encouraging them always to be the best they can. He wants them to grow and excel in whatever they choose to be. Hank wants them to follow their passion and hopes this passion will make them successful. As a baseball icon there are very few players in the history of the game that has equaled what he has done. Hank was tremendously committed to his sport and he always strived to be the best. Like my father, Jackie, he always took on the hard challenges of the game and fought [through] difficult time[s], but through it all they continued to love the game. And the two were never afraid to be who they are and to stand up to what they believed in. I am so happy each and every time I see Hank and his wife Billye. I am also so glad they are a part of our lives. There are so many comparisons between Hank and my father that can be made. For example, besides strength and character, the two were faced with tremendous obstacles. For my father, it was breaking the color barrier and for Hank it was breaking this revered record. Hank and my father stayed focused and they were able to succeed. They were both pioneers with fans that were for them and those that were against them. The two also received so many death threats and again it was their strength of character that won [out for] both. And both Hank and my father never let the information relating to those letters of hate out to their fellow teammates. They did not want it to stand in the way of their team being successful. These two men made us so proud to be African

Americans. My father and Hank helped deliver to us all this wonderful message of commitment and courage. On a personal note one of my most favorite moments occurred during my mother's 90th birthday celebration. I was so delighted to see Hank there and help my mother celebrate this tremendous milestone for our family. After that moment I felt even closer to Hank at that point."

— Sharon Robinson (Daughter of Jackie Robinson)

Atlanta Braves Archives

"Even though my playing days are over I still love going to baseball games even to this day. I also remember growing up and going to Ponce de Leon Park where the Double A Atlanta Crackers used to play. They used to be called the Yankees of the minor leagues because of all of the championships they had won over the years. I remember my dad had season tickets and they were 50 cents apiece and the two of us would go and watch the Atlanta Crackers. And sadly, one of the most vivid memories of that stadium for me growing up were these bleachers they had in right field designated for African American fans. The baseball field was segregated and that is why it is so important for me to talk about Hank Aaron. As Hank went through his minor league playing days he played in many of these southern cities which were segregated; and that is why he was kind of like the Jackie Robinson of the minor leagues.

"Hank Aaron let his bat do the talking. He never wavered and being a fan of the Braves and of Hank Aaron I remember where I was when he hit the home run to pass Babe Ruth. Even though 1974 was not a great year for me politically because I had lost my first election, but I remember watching every game because I wanted Hank to break the record. And when he did break the record, for me he did it in that stereotypical style Hank Aaron was known for. A flick of the wrist and a line drive over the left field fence; and that is how I always remember him hitting the ball. It was such a great night. It was a great moment for Hank Aaron and it was a great moment for baseball.

"On a personal note, Hank Aaron is a wonderful human being. I've known Hank Aaron casually over the years. As I've gotten older I've gotten to know him better. I remember on one occasion I invited him to speak to my staff and interns during one of our quarterly meetings about his career and his life experiences. I invited Hank to one of those meetings and my staff and interns were mesmerized. He spoke about all of the death threats and his quest in breaking the record. He spoke about all of the intimidation and the struggles he faced and again they were all mesmerized. Even though many of those on my staff knew his story but then when you hear about it and all of those experiences firsthand it was a pretty special moment for all of us. Hank Aaron to me is the quintessential living legend and he has been that ever since he hit

Courtesy of the Georgia Sports Hall of Fame

that home run. As a public officer for the state of Georgia and [someone] who has been engaged in politics since Hank Aaron and his playing days, he and that home run has had more of an impact on our community and society in this state than it did for the game of baseball. That legendary home run has had so much impact because of the pressure Hank Aaron had in hitting it and the pressure that was existing in this country at the time and especially down here in the south. Hank Aaron's life and the way he lived it, and his experiences have better helped us all grow together as we all changed together. It is a great pleasure being a part of a great tribute to a great man."

—United States Senator
John Isakson (Georgia)

"Hank Aaron will forever be remembered as the man who broke what some would say [is] sports' greatest record, hitting his 715th homer in 1974. His incredible career as a member of the Atlanta Braves changed the history of my home state team. Not only is he one of the greatest baseball players of all times, but his humanitarian work and commitment to young people have earned him a permanent place in both sports history and American society. During his 23 years of baseball, Hank Aaron paved the way for many great athletes, showing great compassion, vision, and athletic ability. No one has been a better athlete and citizen than Hank Aaron. He is a great American and I'm proud to call him to call him a fellow Georgian."

—United States Senator Saxby Chambliss (Georgia)

"I am honored to share my home state of Alabama with one of baseball's all-time legends. The 40th anniversary of Hank Aaron's home run record marks an important day for our state, but all Americans can be proud of Hank Aaron's accomplishments and contributions to America's game."

—United States Senator Richard Shelby (Alabama)

Courtesy of the Georgia Sports Hall of Fame

"Hank Aaron is a legend for his on-field greatness and his courageousness and leadership in the face of racial unrest. To many he is best known for surpassing Babe Ruth's all-time home run record—one of the greatest sports achievements of all time.

A Mobile native, Hank Aaron has always made Alabama proud. Indeed, the new ballpark, home of the Mobile Bay Bears, is Henry Aaron Stadium. He radiated integrity and strength in the struggle for equality and civil rights. In fact, his success and example played a key role in civil rights progress.

As a boy, the Milwaukee Braves were my favorite team. I followed Hank Aaron and his career closely over the years. He was a hero of mine. I can still name the lineup for the 1957 team that won the World Series. Aaron also had family roots in Wilcox County, where I grew up."

—United States Senator Jeff Sessions (Alabama)

"Like Jackie Robinson before him, Hank Aaron's challenges off the field were greater than those on the field. He responded to those challenges as the gentleman he is, with grace, dignity, and decency. Aaron's legacy stretches far longer than the length of 755 home runs and far beyond the boundaries of the state we both call home. He's a national icon and one of the greatest American athletes in our history. It's fitting that an African American would break Babe Ruth's record in Atlanta, Georgia, the city that produced Martin Luther King Jr. and provided the heartbeat of the civil rights movement. A huge percentage of our state's population today wasn't alive in 1974; but even Georgians who never saw him don a Braves jersey know he's a part of this community because of his humanitarian work. Hank Aaron has seen great success as a Georgia businessman and he continues to give back to the people in this city and in this state. Georgians take great pride that he's one of us."

—Governor Nathan Deal (State of Georgia)

"It is an honor to claim Hank Aaron as an Alabama son. Hank Aaron broke many baseball records during his career. His contributions both on and off the baseball field have made significant impacts in the lives of Alabamians. His legacy has inspired others to chase their own dreams."

—Governor Robert J. Bentley (State of Alabama)

"Henry Aaron was one of the baseball idols of my childhood, when I fell in love with the game. As a kid, I only knew he was a great player. Only later did I realize that he was also a person of great character whose career taught important lessons that transcend baseball. As he approached Babe Ruth's career home run record, he demonstrated some of the same fortitude that Jackie Robinson exhibited when he broke the baseball color barrier.

"The first generation of African-American baseball stars were truly giants, both on and off the field. Those men and others from that era were worthy of the admiration that kids like me had for them. I hope we will see their equals again before too long."

—Supreme Court Justice Samuel Alito

Courtesy of the National Baseball Hall of Fame and Museum

"Hank Aaron helped change the game especially from the cultural standpoint because blacks were the last to make it into the major leagues. At one point there were three leagues—the white league, which was the major league; the Latin American League; and the Negro Leagues. And when the white league (major leagues) opened up to the black players who did come in, they came in as apprentices. Whoever it was—Jackie Robinson, Don Newcombe, Willie Mays, or Hank Aaron—they came in as outsiders, but they already had the same playing capacity and skill as those in the major leagues. Yet, this story repeats itself in other sports for black athletes. Take for example football, where for years blacks were not allowed to play in the same league. Then Marion Motley came along and became an all-star fullback with the Cleveland Browns. In boxing, the story also repeated itself, and it was Jack Johnson who broke barriers in the sport and out of the struggles and obstacles he faced sprang the legacy of Muhammad Ali. These athletes were not only pioneers and they were not just champions but they were also heroes, and there is a difference. A champion is carried on the backs and shoulders of the people and a hero carries the people on his back. That is why a hero doesn't happen and come along every night. Hank Aaron was a hero because he kept on striving and competing in a sport that told him that he couldn't and wasn't supposed to succeed. And Hank Aaron did this in a midst of threats and the danger that he faced. It is amazing how a game that is supposed to be so objective, which features a pitching mound 60 feet and 6 inches from the plate and bases that are 90 feet from each other, could show such barbarism and racial thoughts. But, because Hank Aaron kept moving forward and because he kept swinging he helped redefine the game for us all. Hank is as much a hero on the field as he is off the field. As for who was the greatest player that has ever played the game all I can say is, there is room at the top of the mountain. There is room for many and there are many who are on that mountain that are now in baseball heaven. Hank is on that mountain, and he is standing beside players like Josh Gibson, Jackie Robinson, Barry Bonds, Willie Mays, Ted Williams, and Joe DiMaggio. The mountain is not like a tip and it is not like a needle; that is why there is room at the top of the mountain for many. So, it is hard to say who is the best. Hank has been a very good friend. Hank is also a very decent man and I can honestly proclaim this because I've known him and [I have] been his friend for more than 40 years. He is socially conscious

and civic-minded. He is also extremely aware of social justice. Henry relates to everyone, young and old. Henry Aaron is a social activist and a hero to his effort. Henry has been on my Board for years. I remember he came to one function many years back during his playing days to speak to the group. There he met a sick little boy and he promised to hit a home run for him, like a Babe Ruth-like story. Henry did one better and he ended up hitting two home runs that day against the Cubs. These are the types of stories where heroes are made. What always amazed me was that Henry never got the attention he so rightfully deserved during his playing days. Henry always came off looking average, but in reality he was extraordinary. A lot of that attention or lack of attention happened because of where Henry played. He didn't play in New York or in California, so he wasn't logistically going to get the praise he so rightfully deserved if he were playing in another market. Atlanta and Milwaukee are not the markets one generally considered as large media markets. But that didn't stop Henry Aaron from consistently hitting home runs and helping his team win ball games. Henry is an amazing person and a remarkable human being and I am extremely proud to be able to call him my friend."

—Reverend Jesse Jackson (American civil rights activist and Baptist minister. He was also a candidate for the Democratic presidential nomination in 1984 and 1988.)

"Hank Aaron's legacy extends beyond the baseball field. His record-breaking career shattered racial stereotypes and barriers, and showed the nation and the world the power of hard work and perseverance in the face of daunting obstacles. Here in Atlanta, Hank Aaron continues to make a lasting impact on our city, and we are honored and privileged to be a part of his incredible American story. He taught us all that no matter what life throws at you just keep swinging."

—Mayor Kasim Reed (Atlanta, Georgia)

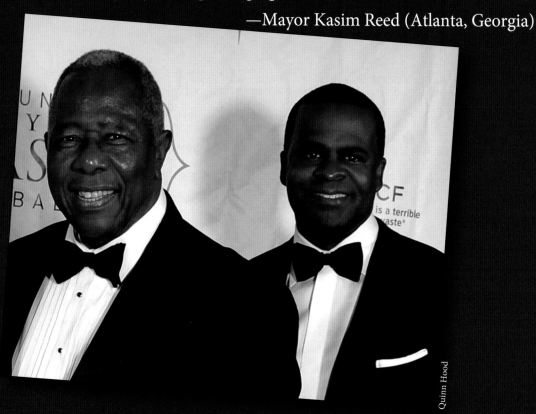

Quinn Hood

City of Mobile Archives

"Hank Aaron and I are very good friends. I know he really loves his hometown. Hank visits all of the time for various functions and I think he particularly enjoys watching his town grow into a great city. The people of Mobile, Alabama are very close. In fact, Hank's brother James and I were fellow classmates in high school. So, I've known the Aarons almost my entire life. I knew his parents and I can certainly understand why Hank is such a great and super guy because of his parents. Hank has this amazing character. It's like a magnet that always draws people closer to him. But on the other hand Hank is so modest. He remains one of the greatest players that have ever played the game of baseball, and he is certainly proud of that, but it is not the first thing he wants to talk to you about. When he talks to people he seems more interested in hearing and learning about their life experiences and situations. Hank is especially concerned about society in general. In Mobile, we have Hank Aaron and his home, which they have turned into a museum, and we are very proud of that. I also know the town itself still gets very excited when they know he's here visiting or on official business because to the citizens of Mobile he is a positive ambassador for our town. Hank really enjoys that reputation wherever he goes. Hank always promotes and encourages others to do well. I know he spent a long time in Atlanta and Milwaukee during his playing days, but I kind of think this town of Mobile, Hank's hometown, has helped develop the character and the man we know today. Hank has always been proud to be from Mobile and we will always be proud of him."

—Mayor Samuel Jones (Mobile, Alabama)

"This is one interview I didn't have to prepare for because I am a big sports fan and especially a big Hank Aaron fan! I am truly a baseball fan. I've met Hank Aaron on several occasions whether I was in the capacity of mayor of Milwaukee or during my time in Congress. But, for me, I grew up when Hank Aaron played for the Braves when they were here in Milwaukee. I remember I grew up only a mile and a half from the stadium. I used to hang out there all of the time growing up. In fact, in that last year when the Braves were in Milwaukee I went to 31 games that year! It was 50 cents a ticket and it was the place to go. I remember even going to the stadium all the time with my buddies. My parents would drop us off for the game. Then when the game was over they would pick us up. I remember I got into so much trouble with my dad because I went to the last game the Braves were in town because I didn't come out of the stadium right away. I was one of those crazy fans who were running around the field at the end of the game.

"Hank Aaron was bigger than life for me. And, growing up I used to play right field just like Hank Aaron, but as I got older I realized I was playing right field for a number of other different reasons. I remember watching Hank Aaron running so effortlessly and gracefully. I saw in

him this great right fielder and not just a great home run hitter. Hank Aaron was an overall great ballplayer and besides that he was such a great role model for those who followed his play. Hank Aaron was someone we all looked up to. And even today, he continues to be a great role model and he continues to do it effortlessly and gracefully. My experiences with him beginning the first time we met was someone who is a great gentleman, soft spoken and always kind to people. He is not someone who has sought out the limelight every chance he gets. He continues to visit Milwaukee every year. In fact, Milwaukee hosts a run in his honor every year. As a baby boomer I have the utmost admiration for Hank Aaron which runs very deep. Fittingly, Hank Aaron began and finished his career in Milwaukee. Again, my most vivid memory growing up as a kid was watching this tremendously talented right fielder play in the city that I have always called home."

—Mayor Tom Barrett (Milwaukee, Wisconsin)

"I can't imagine a person with a heavier burden then Hank Aaron when he was approaching Babe Ruth's home run record. We like to imagine that since the Civil Rights Act was signed in the 1960s that we are somehow living in some kind of post-racial world. The 3000 pieces of hate mail that Hank Aaron was receiving as he was approaching the 714 home run record set by Babe Ruth is a testament to the struggles that Hank Aaron had to overcome. To put it in simple words, baseball is a sport that is about hitting a ball with a bat, and yet it remains as one of the hardest things to do in all of sports. It requires a tremendous amount of skill, talent, and athleticism, but then if you imagine all of the hate that was directed at Hank Aaron and then to overcome this opposition really represents a significant milestone. And, it wasn't the mark of 714 home runs, but rather when Hank Aaron hit that 715th home run it really means the most to me and shows, to me, how he sent the United States out beyond where it already existed. Hank Aaron sent that home run into the future. Hank Aaron sent that ball, not over the fence, and not just to set the record for himself and his team, but he sent it out there to help the rest of us to move further along as a nation on the difficult path that we have been on since 1619 when the first slaves came to America, a year before the Pilgrims landed at Plymouth Rock. Like Jackie Robinson before him, Hank Aaron carried as big a baseball burden as any other baseball player was expected to carry. No other athlete, besides Jackie Robinson, was required to carry this burden as much as Hank Aaron and he did it with such grace and professionalism. I think that Hank Aaron brings to this record all of the modesty and dignity that one person can bring. It is just another tribute to one of the most extraordinary Americans that has ever lived. I had the great privilege to meet and know Hank Aaron. I consider him one of the great heroes, not just to this glorious game of baseball, but in all of American history. It is interesting when you enter into discussions as to who were the greatest players, who have ever played this game, and once you get past Babe Ruth, then you can have an interesting argument. And, it doesn't matter where you are—at the stadium, at a friend's house, at the bar—there [are] always discussions, and rightfully so, that Hank Aaron is one of the greatest along with Willie Mays, Barry Bonds, Mickey Mantle, Joe DiMaggio, Ted Williams. . . . It is always a very small crowd that is considered the greatest. Hank Aaron certainly deserves to be a part of those discussions as being one of the greatest players that has ever played this game.

"We know that Hank Aaron hit 755 home runs in a sport when numbers mean so much. If I were to ask the average fan how many yards rushing did Walter Payton have? Or, how many passing yards did Dan Marino have for his career? No one can answer that, but in baseball numbers matter; 300 wins mean something, a .406 batting average means something, 56 consecutive games with a hit means something, and 714 and 755 home runs means something. I am a huge baseball fan and a student of this remarkable game. That is why 755 home runs means so much to me because it is synonymous with Hank Aaron. And, to think Hank Aaron was one of the last Negro Leagues players who came into the major leagues to retire, it starts to help connect him to the whole history of this game in this country and the history of the Jim Crow Laws, and slavery, and the Civil Rights Act. Those 755 home runs make for such a powerful message and the gravity that home run did for us all. I've read some of those hate letters and death threats that were sent to Hank Aaron during his quest for the record. They are shocking knowing that it only happened in the United States just 40 years ago. That is why Hank Aaron is such a significant individual in baseball and in the healing of our country."
—Ken Burns (Award-winning filmmaker and Director/Emmy Award-winning and groundbreaking filmmaker of the documentary *Baseball*.)

Courtesy of the National Baseball Hall of Fame and Museum

"Hank was a champion slugger who gave us one of the happiest days in a tumultuous decade. He and I were born in the same year, and I've always admired people with two first names."

—Garry Marshall (Legendary producer and Hollywood icon)

"Hank Aaron to me represents excellence, but understated excellence because he might not have hit 60 home runs in a season and he didn't make the flair for the dramatic like so many other players. All he did was to show up for work and be consistently excellent for years and years—and if you know anything about baseball, that is a very difficult thing to do. So, if I had to make a short sentence, that consistency, and being understated helped define who Hank Aaron is. As a man, Hank Aaron is one of the most decent human beings around. There are so many aspects to Hank Aaron, especially when he was about to shatter Babe Ruth's home run record. It is also amazing to think about his career and the adversity and obstacles he faced. Baseball is a game that is all about numbers. If I said to you '56,' you as a baseball fan would know exactly what I mean and what I am talking about. The way that Hank Aaron went about his business has always impressed me. For so many years, the consistency this man demonstrated, it is almost hard to believe. I would be remiss if I didn't mention when we were making the movie *42* and you get so immersed in this stuff, but I had the opportunity to read some of the letters that were written to both these men. And what is so unimaginable to me is here you are a good and decent person who is doing what one should do at the highest level, but because of the color of your skin you receive these indescribable letters. You are getting these death threats that are directed at you and even your family from strangers who are so ignorant about their feelings that they seem as though they have to convey their feelings through a letter. It's not like today when someone can post an anonymous post on social media. Back in the 1970s it took a lot of effort to send a threatening letter.

"After I read some of the letters it made me so profoundly glad to know that Hank is such a great friend. I think there are a lot of complexities as to what Hank Aaron went through compared in some ways to Jackie Robinson, who too received this large amount of hate mail and threats. The other thing that is interesting to me is a story told to me by Ken Griffey Jr., another good friend of mine. He said, 'Whenever I attend special occasions or events like the All Star Game and when the Hall of Famers came by it was always so amazing and then when Hank Aaron enters the room everyone there stands up a little taller.' I know this might sound like a cliché, but when you meet someone you have always looked up to or have read so much about and you think of them as this modern-day hero and all of those things that person might not be the person you think they are, but Hank Aaron is everything you ever hoped he is. Hank Aaron is a great friend, and every time I talk or meet with him I am in awe and that feeling never goes away. There is no question I feel like I am living a dream. I feel like I am an observer of history.

"Let me tell you a story, which should demonstrate the power and reach of Hank Aaron. We were filming a portion of the film *42* down in Atlanta and Hank was kind enough to visit the set one day. I gotta tell you something, from Harrison Ford to the extras on the set, they all lost their minds and you could feel it when they saw Hank Aaron in person. It just helps to illustrate that [it is] not just those in the sports world who understand the importance [of] Hank Aaron, but that his reach is extremely unique and he is universal. I was also at the National Baseball Hall of Fame recently at an event, and I noticed that when Hank Aaron came into the room things were different even considering there were other Hall of Fame members present. I am truly the luckiest guy you'd ever want to meet in your life and that is absolutely for sure and I am so grateful to be a part of this book and appreciate the tone and the level of respect it demonstrates  for Hank Aaron. And, I'll end on this note, I feel like Hank Aaron perhaps is finally getting the respect and admiration he deserves because of all of the controversy involving steroids that history will allow us to look back and examine all that he did for this sport. And, because Hank Aaron was not a self-promoter I feel like more young players, fans, and people are beginning to realize what this man is all about and what this man stands for because it is certainly a story worth telling."

—Thomas Tull (American businessman and film producer. He is currently the Chairman of the Board and Chief Executive Officer [CEO] of Legendary Pictures.)

# Hall of Fame Class

"Hank Aaron was a quiet man and yet he played the game at a level few have ever played it at all. Hank played at a level that made a lot of pitchers feel unhappy . . . myself included. I never expected to get Hank Aaron out all of the times or maybe not ever. Hank was one of those batters you make sure you get the batters in front of him out as often as you could. This way you could lessen the damage when he eventually comes up. Now, that we are both retired and are both Hall of Famers I do get to see him in these types of situations as opposed to facing him in the batter's box. I prefer that meeting much better. Hank has always been a quiet man, and he still is. Hank is both gracious and cordial. Hank has always played this game without being flashy and he always got the job done. He's kind of like Teddy Roosevelt though . . . Hank has always spoken softly and he carried a very big stick."

—Sandy Koufax (National Baseball Hall of Fame Member, class of 1972)

"To me Hank Aaron is one of the top five players this game has ever seen. I personally wish I had more of an opportunity to play against him. He was always in the other league most of his career and there was no such thing as interleague play back then. I used to marvel at the way he played the game and I think he is an underrated all-around player. Hank Aaron was a great outfielder, he ran the bases well, he was a great base runner, and of course he was a great, great home run hitter. Hank Aaron is one of those special guys that have played this game and he continues to be a credit to this game."

—Al Kaline (National Baseball Hall of Fame Member, class of 1980)

Georgia Sports Hall of Fame

"When I think of Hank Aaron, I think of someone who was a consummate profession-al. He was the type of player that I tried to measure up to on and off the field. On the field, he made everything look so simple. He could throw, he could hit, and he could steal a base if he had to (or wanted to). He made it all look so easy. When I played him, I tried to do everything he did. If he hit a home run, I'd try to hit a home run. If he hit two home runs, I'd try to hit two home runs. If he hit three home runs, I'd see him the next day at the ballpark!"

—Frank Robinson (National Baseball Hall of Fame Member, class of 1982)

Courtesy of the National Baseball Hall of Fame and Museum

"When I think of Hank Aaron I think about one of the most fantastic players this game has ever seen and the Home Run King. I know there is always some controversy as to who is the greatest but Hank is certainly one of the greatest players, along with Mays, Mantle, and Frank Robinson. I guess whoever you want to be the greatest is the greatest. Hank Aaron is a guy who could do everything the game demanded. I literally like the way he has always handled himself. For example, through all of the controversy when Barry Bonds was hitting all of those homeruns. But to be honest, I don't even think about Bonds anymore because I know Hank was the greatest. I do believe when the dust eventually settles down most fans will think of only Hank as the true all-time Home Run King. I also know about the struggles many of these players had during their playing days knowing Frank Robinson as well as I did. I remember witnessing the segregation issues for myself. I remember the days you used to play in cities like Kansas City and African American ballplayers couldn't stay in Kansas City, Missouri but rather they had to travel to Kansas City, Kansas to stay in a hotel. Even as late as 1959, I remember team members having to stay in two different hotels. It was such a different mindset those days but Henry faced all of these challenges and he overcame them and that is the example of the greatness in him. To me, I respect Henry so much and he has always been a great friend over the years."

—Brooks Robinson (National Baseball Hall of Fame Member, class of 1983)

"Henry Aaron was such a great guy and a good teammate and his records are certainly unmatched. He played this game and did what he did to get the job done. Henry could do whatever this game demanded and he did it with class and grace. He was a solid ballplayer, he was a great base runner, fielder, and of course his hitting spoke for itself. Henry was an all-around great ballplayer and one of the best this game has seen. He was a great student of the game and he knew this game so well. I was also impressed how Henry would often use the entire field when he hit. Despite what they say about 'you gotta hit the ball up the middle to be successful.' He used the whole field and that is what made him such a dangerous hitter. He used to hit from line to line depending on the situation. It always seemed like he could place the ball wherever he wanted. If you ask any baseball player who has ever played with Henry about his hitting, you are going to hear them say he was outstanding. If you asked them about his fielding you are going to hear the same response. And, if you asked them about his running ability again you are probably going to hear the same response about Henry being outstanding or any other number of words that would emphasize the remarkable player that he was when he played this game. Henry was just an all-around great ballplayer and a great guy to be around. We were very close as fellow players and as a team in Milwaukee. We were all focused as a team and Henry was one of the leaders. He never said he was the leader but we all knew he was. Henry led by example. When the ballgame was over Henry usually was a part of every win. It might not have been a hit or a home run but it might have been a play in the field he was involved in, or a base he stole to set up the winning run. Henry was a winner."

—Red Schoendienst (National Baseball Hall of Fame Member, class of 1989)

"How do I feel about Hank Aaron? Well . . . I kind of talked about him at the National Baseball Hall of Fame during my Induction Ceremony in 1990. I remember mentioning how I would always strive to do as well as I could in the game I played because of the guys who were sitting behind me at the time on stage during the ceremony. All I knew is they were big shoes to fill knowing the likes of Hank Aaron, Joe DiMaggio, Ted Williams, Stan Musial, Early Wynn, Bob Lemon, Sandy Koufax were just a few of the greats in attendance that day. They were some of the greatest players that have ever played this game and I respected and looked up to each and every one of them and I almost felt unworthy of the praise I was receiving at the time. I remember pitching against Hank Aaron when I hit the big leagues when I was nineteen years old. It was during spring training when the Orioles traveled to play the Braves. I also remember becoming really good friends with Dusty Baker, who was great friends with Hank Aaron and then of course went on to have all of those great years with Tommy Lasorda in Los Angeles as well as several other ball clubs. We would often talk about the game and he told me that he owed his success to Hank Aaron. Dusty told me that Hank taught him everything about the game and he was never afraid to share his knowledge and that was the type of person Hank was. For me, I faced Hank more at the twilight of his career when he came back and played for the Milwaukee Brewers of the American League.

"Hank was so humble and he was such a good all-around player. These are some of the qualities and dynamics that made Hank such a great ballplayer. Hank made it look so easy, but being a ballplayer is more than that. Hank Aaron is one of those players who devoted so much time to this game and as a result this has made him such a great role model for all players to aspire to.

"I've met Hank Aaron on several occasions and meeting him is always like meeting someone that is royalty. Especially because of the way he carries himself. Hank is dignified and humble, [extremely] talented, and is certainly the type of person you want representing the game, and for me that is very important."

—Jim Palmer (National Baseball
      Hall of Fame Member class
            of 1990)

Atlanta Braves Archives

"I have always been a huge fan of Hank Aaron growing up. I remember I grew up and lived in Panama and everyone played baseball every day. It was the sport we played. And, all of the boys back then were either Dodgers or Yankees fans. I, on the other hand, was a Milwaukee Braves fan. I was a fan primarily because of Hank Aaron. I remember reading the papers as much as I could when I was younger as my way of following the Braves and Hank Aaron. Then I remember meeting Hank Aaron for the first time at the very first All Star Game I played in and I thought about how special that moment and the game then meant to me. Meeting Hank Aaron meant a lot to me knowing that he was one of my idols as a young boy in Panama. I remember standing next to him and in this quiet demeanor he said 'hello' and I felt like a little boy in Panama again. Thank you Hank!"

—Rod Carew (National Baseball Hall of Fame Member, class of 1991)

Courtesy of the Minnesota Twins

"I thought Hank was one of the greatest home run hitters I faced. I was fortunate enough that he only hit two home runs against me, and I faced him for 11 years. The great amount of respect right-handed pitchers had for him came from the fact that he was a line drive, home run hitter... if you made a mistake, the pitch was going to be done. Kids in the outfield stands were going to be playing with that ball. When I look back at the years I played against him, I had a lot of respect for him."

—Ferguson "Fergie" Jenkins (National Baseball Hall of Fame Member, class of 1991)

"When the Houston Astros hosted my retirement party with the organization the club's owner, Jim Crane, flew Hank Aaron in for the event. I remember Henry gave the best speech I ever heard him give . . . of course, I'm a little biased knowing that Henry said a lot of nice things about me! Henry spoke about how he used to listen to me on the radio while growing up and how I helped teach him the game of baseball. He also mentioned how, every time he hears the call of his 715th home run and hears my voice, we are somehow connected. I remember I had all winter to think about how I was going to describe the home run when he did hit it. There was so much excitement on that April 8, 1974 day. People often ask me if I was nervous that day. I would tell them I was so busy I didn't have a chance to be nervous and think about how I was going to call Aaron's record-breaking home run. I remember I did the six o'clock news sports segment that day. I had to do the pre-game show, and I was on the field set to do the opening ceremonies. So again, I didn't have the time to be nervous. And besides, why should we be nervous? We all knew Henry was going to break the record. It was just a matter of when.

"Henry and I actually go way back. I even got to call his first home run when I was working for the Cardinals. He hit it off of Vic Raschi in 1954. Henry and I had a wonderful relationship over the years. I can't describe how proud I was to call Henry's record-breaking home run and I will always remember the words I used. I said, 'There's a new home run champion of all time . . . and it's Henry Aaron!' I remember the Braves organization did it right and how they handled the Aaron march to the record; whereas the Yankees didn't handle it well when it came to Maris when he broke the single-season mark of 61 home runs in 1961. Henry, on the other hand, was such a great mentor, especially for the younger players. And of course, he was one of the greatest of all time. Yet it is so difficult to label a player and their placement as to who was the best. Let's just say, if you were to pick the top five ballplayers of all time, in no particular order, and put them on a list, then Henry Aaron would be on that list. I was so proud to be a part of this moment in baseball history. Again, I had all winter to think about what I was going to say and I also had all winter to think about what I wasn't going to say. Meaning, over the years, one of my catch phrases was always, 'Holy Toledo!' when someone hit a home run. It's something I've said since the 1950s when I broke into the minor leagues. But, I told myself, when Henry did hit the

Courtesy of the Houston Astros

48

record-breaking home run I wasn't going to say 'Holy Toledo!' because it was always going to be Henry's moment and not mine."

—Milo Hamilton (National Baseball Hall of Fame Ford C. Frick Member, class of 1992)

"I was shocked when someone told me that Henry Aaron only hit .220 off of me. I thought it was at least 100 points higher. I just hated to see him come up, especially in a key situation. I can't imagine too many pitchers over his career actually like pitching to Henry. His bat was so quick across the plate. He wasn't an overly big guy but he was so powerfully built. It is remarkable that he hit 755 home runs and not once did he hit 50 in a season."

—Tom Seaver (National Baseball Hall of Fame Member, class of 1992)

Georgia Sports Hall of Fame

Atlanta Braves Archives

"Of all players I faced in my 17 years, Hank Aaron ranks as one of the three greatest players I ever faced. His only inside-the-park home run came off me at Connie Mack Stadium, the only home run he got off me. Don Lock was our centerfielder. Hank hit a line drive over my head and Lock tried to make a diving catch. The ball got by him and rolled all the way to the centerfield wall. It was the hardest ball he hit off me. You can check the numbers and he didn't get many hits off me. But I was lucky to have that type of success off of him. Not too many pitchers can probably say that. I just wouldn't throw anything hard to him, all garbage . . . change-ups, slow curves—and always I was able to keep the ball down."

—Jim Bunning (National Baseball Hall of Fame Member, class of 1996)

"Hank Aaron was a great player. All that Hank Aaron was concerned about was playing the game right, playing it to the best of his ability, winning games for his team, and to me being the greatest home run hitter this game has ever seen. I've known Hank for years. I remember playing against him when he played for the Jacksonville Braves in the South Atlantic League and then I pitched against him in Puerto Rico when he was down there. Henry could hit off of any pitcher and as a pitcher I found out how good he was pretty quickly. No matter who you were as a pitcher you weren't safe on the mound when it came to facing Henry Aaron. Hank was such a great player and when you get to know him as well as I you realize what a great guy he really is. Henry is so humble and so nice. Every time we are together all we ever do is just laugh. It is always a nice warm feeling every time I run into him. Henry never was cheated out of a swing and he was so patient and he was just this model of consistency. I remember the day when he hit the home run to break Babe Ruth's record. I was the third base coach for the Dodgers at the time. I remember there was so much excitement that day. I can recall how Bill Buckner, who was playing left field for us, climbed the fence to catch the ball from going over the fence and then how Tom House grabbed the ball in the bullpen. I really thought Henry wanted to wait until he got back to Atlanta to break the record in front of the home crowd and for his sake he did. I think Henry is one of those stars that only comes around every generation. And, because of how great he was, Henry made the players around him so much better. But for me, what I will always remember about Henry Aaron is how we laugh every time we are together. He's such a great guy and his wife is the salt of the Earth. Henry will always mean the world to me and he will always be an inspiration to me."

—Tommy Lasorda (National Baseball Hall of Fame Member, class of 1997)

"People all over the world followed Hank Aaron and even more became fans as he approached the home run record in 1974. So many fans wanted to see Henry break the record and sadly there were many who didn't want to see him break the record. The thing that amazed me the most about Henry was that he didn't let any of the negative criticism affect his play or  he  didn't let on to his team that this was going on. As he was approaching the record I do remember Henry couldn't stay at the same hotels as the rest of the team. He couldn't go to the stadiums when the rest of us traveled there. He had to sneak in and out so much because of the criticism from those who didn't want to see him break Babe Ruth's record. And then, Henry was getting all of those death threats and I'm not sure if as few as five guys on the ballclub ever knew about any of those threats; and those threats were real. Henry hid it so well. I didn't even know about the threats or any of this was going on. I found out about it afterwards. I remember there were some books that had just come out and then there were articles I found in the newspapers after the fact and I said to myself, 'You gotta be kidding! He went through all of that?'  You wouldn't even know it because that is the kind of guy Henry is and what kind of teammate he was. Henry is so quiet and soft-spoken and he never let the media or any of the criticism or the threats get in the way of what was going on in the club house or on the field. Henry kept this from us because he also respected our privacy and he didn't want the team to be affected in any negative way. But as that April 1974 day did approach we as a team all knew it was going to happen and the record would be broken. It was inevitable. The only question was 'When will it happen?' 'Which team

will it be hit off of and which pitcher?' and 'Ultimately, how far was Henry going to hit it?' As team members you would stand and visualize these types of things. What most people don't know is that I was Henry's teammate and played alongside of him longer than any other player. Longer than Eddie Mathews, or Warren Spahn, or any of those guys. My best recollection of Henry was when he used to come to the ballpark. I used to watch how he put on his uniform, and then how he went out and took batting practice, and then how he took his infield practice each and every day he played the game. Henry was never flashy, he never did any showboating, and he never sought the spotlight. Henry Aaron just went out and played the game the way the game should be played."

—Phil Niekro (National Baseball Hall of Fame Member, class of 1997)

"I remember the first time as a pitcher I faced Hank Aaron. We all knew who Hank Aaron was. Any kid that followed baseball and loved the game, which I was, knew who Hank Aaron was. We knew he was one of the class players in baseball. I remember when I first faced him, he probably already had 400-plus home runs and I went into the clubhouse and asked Don Drysdale how I should pitch to Hank Aaron. Drysdale replied, 'You gotta bust him inside, bust him inside, and then a slider down and away.' I then said, 'But Big D . . . I don't throw a slider!' Then Drysdale responded, 'Then go and take your uniform off. You're not pitching today!' That is how my introduction on how to pitch to Hank Aaron came about. The first time we faced each other I think he got me twice for a few hits, one of them might have been a home run, and then I got him out twice. I think I might have won that first game against him. I will always remember something I read in the newspaper shortly after that first encounter. They asked Hank Aaron what he thought about the Dodgers' new kid as a pitcher (meaning myself). Hank said, 'He comes right at you. He doesn't back down for anyone.' So, when Hank Aaron throws around a compliment such as that you can feel pretty good about yourself. But it was more a thrill than a fight to face a guy who was one of the greatest and who went on to be the game's all-time home run hitter. It was a privilege to be on the same field with him over the years. I think we had a few more battles, but I will always remember that first encounter with Hank Aaron."

Courtesy of the Atlanta Braves

—Don Sutton (National Baseball Hall of
Fame Member, class of 1998)

"Hank Aaron is a perfect gentleman. He exemplifies what a major league ballplayer should be. Without a doubt Hank Aaron is a class act. All of the things he had to endure and the way he did it highlights what kind of class act he is. I see him every year in Cooperstown at the National Baseball Hall of Fame and sadly that is all I ever see [of] him. I was fortunate to play against him for a very short period of time at the end of his career but still he is a class act on and off the field."

—George Brett (National Baseball Hall of Fame Member, class of 1999)

Atlanta Braves Archives

"The one thing that I always admired about Henry is that he played the game the way it should be. The funny thing for me was you could never tell if Henry was having a good day or a bad day. His temperament and his approach to the game was the same every day; day in and day out. And, from my perspective that is what you look for in a true professional. Henry was always one of those unique players who was not just a great hitter but he was also a great power hitter. He had this very controlled swing and a good eye at the plate. So, whenever I had to face him offensively to me Henry was the total package. Over the years I never paid attention to that many situations but it was always a real challenge to face him on those occasions. As a pitcher you

Georgia Sports Hall of Fame

never had a comfort level when you had to face Henry Aaron. On a personal note I used to follow his career when I was a teenager and when he played for the Milwaukee Braves. In fact, I had to face Henry Aaron in one of my very first games ever when I made it to the big leagues. I was just nineteen years old and I was with the New York Mets and the game was in Shea Stadium. I was called into the game from the bullpen to face Henry and his Atlanta Braves that also included Joe Torre, Eddie Mathews, and all of those great players. I guess you can say I was thrown into the proverbial fire very early."

—Nolan Ryan (National Baseball Hall of Fame Member, class of 1999)

Courtesy of the Houston Astros

"Hank Aaron and I played on the same team for two years. It was Hank's last two seasons in the big leagues and it was my second and third seasons in the game with the Milwaukee Brewers. Needless to say, Hank Aaron was a very positive influence, not only over my playing career but in my life. There was nothing Hank taught me to do that mechanically made me a better ballplayer, like put your hands this way or shift your weight that way. It was just that he was just another one of the guys on the team. Meaning, here is unquestionably one of the best players this game has ever seen, and he was just this great teammate. And from the standpoint of this young, impressionable nineteen-year-old who had just made it into the big leagues it was so cool to experience him as just another player doing everything he could do to help us win ball games. The rest of the team knew how great a player he was, but the way he carried himself allowed us to relax around him and treat him like a fellow teammate. Hank was just like another one of the guys. Hank treated me, a nineteen-year-old kid, the same way he treated a twenty-year veteran. Hank was extremely humble and he would often hang out with us like any other player . . . yet most of us were young players who made up the team. He never wanted us to treat him any differently, other than the fact he always seemed to have a lot more media than the rest of us. But anyway, we weren't really that good as a team at that time, we were still developing as a team and I'd rather talk to the Home Run King if I were them too. Unfortunately, I didn't get the opportunity to see Hank play at the prime of his career but I do remember following his career when I was growing up. And then, to have the opportunity to be his teammate at a very young age was the greatest impact on my career. I quickly realized that as players we are all in this together and everyone is here for the same reason and that is to win a baseball game and then it really doesn't matter who you are.

"On a personal note, Hank's view of me is always a little embellished because he always seems to give me the greatest compliments. When he talked about me as a nineteen-year-old he gave me so much credit at the time but I didn't think I was that good back then. But, I guess Hank thought I'd figure this game out. Maybe he was just good at seeing potential! Hank always gives me far better compliments than I deserve. We always have a great time together especially when you throw in Bob Uecker. From the standpoint of the famous home run I will also always remember that hit he had off of Al Downing and then watching Tom House catching the ball. As a fan, I was so excited about him breaking the record and all of the accolades leading up to that moment. Hank Aaron is a hell of a great guy!"

—Robin Yount (National Baseball Hall of Fame Member, class of 1999)

Atlanta Braves Archives

"I know Hank, and I played against him for a lot of years. I never played on the same team as Hank but I just remember all of the home runs he hit against us! He was an amazing guy and fortunately for me I got to know him better when I was elected myself into the Hall of Fame. Hank is a classy guy and I always have a great time when I get the chance to spend time with him."

—Tony Perez
(National Baseball Hall of Fame Member, class of 2000)

Atlanta Braves Archives

"Hank Aaron and Willie Mays were two of the Major League Baseball icons from my childhood that I looked up to. As a youngster in the 1970s I had the greatest pleasures playing against both men. I played a few more years against Mr. Aaron. Initially just being on the same field of grass and dirt was at the time to me a supreme achievement. But to watch Hank Aaron approach getting to that magic number of 715 home runs was a thrill. His slow walk to home plate, bat propped between his legs as he donned his helmet. A firm stance in the batter's box, sweat glistening off his . . . forearms as he awaited the pitch. Pitchers almost begging the umpire for a strike zone a little larger since they were facing baseball's best. No such luck. I saw a number of his line drives arch just over the outfield wall with just that quick flick of the wrists, as his weight had shifted to his left foot on the front side. It was over in a moment, like the flick of a light switch. Whenever we played the Atlanta Braves I worked for our team to win the contest, but I wanted Hank to hit one out of the park. I wanted to bear witness to a historical milestone in my chosen sport. Equally as important, I wanted to see a black man eclipse the venerable Babe Ruth in his journey because it would be done in the face of blatant, overt racism. Remember, it was still an era and in a place where this frame of mind and actions were an accepted way of life for many. Hank moved past it in style, with the ease and graciousness he carried throughout his playing days and into his post-career life. With Hank, it was actions that always spoke louder than words. I've gotten to know Hank very well over the years and it's always been an honor and thrill to be with him because I know what he went through to become the Home Run King, and I know he did it the right way. No compromises. He has always carried himself with a great deal of respect and dignity and I love him for that. Hank, live long and live well because you're an inspiration to me and for generations of people."

—Dave Winfield (National Baseball Hall of Fame Member, class of 2001)

"Hank Aaron is a man that has exemplified the qualities of a champion both on and off the field. A man of integrity, pride, and the garnering of respect with the way he has carried himself. May God continue to bless him and his family with good health."

—Ozzie Smith (National Baseball Hall of Fame Member, class of 2002)

"Hank was a great man! And yet what most people don't realize is that he might have been the best overall player of all time who still doesn't get that acknowledgement. Hank could run, he could field, and of course he could hit. He could do it all. Hank put up numbers and was able to perform even given all of the threats which just shows me how strong a man he was, and yet I believe having his name in the middle of the lineup each day and helping his team by striking fear into the opposing team was the most important thing to Hank Aaron. You really got to take your hat off to Hank! He was certainly one of the greatest."

—Eddie Murray (National Baseball Hall of Fame Member, class of 2003)

"Henry is one of the biggest names in this game. Always has and always will [be]. What he did and when he did it was something insurmountable by many that have followed this game. It's funny, back in 1962 you don't look at a fellow teammate and say, 'Someday this guy is going to be the next Home Run King.' Nobody could have predicted that, but Henry was so different and maybe I shouldn't have been surprised. Henry wasn't necessarily the great power hitter when he broke into the game, but he was always this great hitter. Then he made himself into one of the greatest power hitters because Henry could do it. Henry started out as an infielder within the organization and then they converted him to an outfielder. And then he simply went on to become one of the greatest defensive outfielders there was and then he turned out to be the home run champion. Fortunately, I had the opportunity to be with Henry early on with the Braves in Milwaukee and then in Atlanta. I was then the announcer with the Brewers when Henry came back to play his last two years in the big leagues. I even got to call his last home run, number 755, from the booth. It was pretty special calling that last home run Henry ever hit. And through it all we have remained great friends ever since. Yet recently, Henry is pretty mad [at] me. You see, they recently put up a statue of me at Miller Park in Milwaukee and it stands next to Henry's statue and he has accused me of bringing down the real estate value over there. But in all seriousness, it is pretty special to hold the same honor as Henry, along with Robin Yount and the Commissioner of Baseball Bud Selig, with fellow statues at Miller Park.

"It always impressed me how Henry never made a big deal about how good he was, but he could have. What I always did get a kick out of was when we played and when the rest of us mere mortals would go up and ask Henry what kind of pitcher was out there on the mound or ask him, 'How's he throwing out there?' Henry would always say, 'He's got nothing!' and then you'd go out there and the pitcher's throwing 97 mph and has this awesome curveball and then he punches you out on three pitches. Henry was one of those guys who just never gave the opposing pitcher that much credit. Not because he wasn't a good pitcher, but rather that was the way he was. We had a lot of great times together and Henry loved to laugh. And, he loved to laugh a lot. I remember the two of us had lockers next to each other for a while. And, I remember these commercial spots we did together for Magnavox in Milwaukee. I especially remember this spot we were supposed to do for the pregame show and for the [majority] of the time we had to start over because all we did was laugh. I think it took 30 minutes to do a 30-second commercial spot.

"But, you can never appreciate Henry unless you had the opportunity to see him play every day and what he did on a daily basis. Not that he had a thousand hits each year. It was just the way he did the things he did. One night it may have been a great play in the field or the next night it was getting that extra base on a hit to the outfield while on first. Henry could do it all and that is why for the most part when you mention the name 'Henry Aaron' all that most fans want to talk about are all of the home runs he hit. But, because of the things he did besides the home runs, that is why Henry was the total package and when you were his teammate you could appreciate him so much more. When I first joined the Braves we had this great team. There was Mathews, Spahn, Burdette, Torre, Adcock, and Henry, just to name a few. It was a great team that included great hitting and great pitching. I could go on and on how good they were and Henry was a big part of that success. It was just a heck of a ballclub! And back then, so many of us lived in Milwaukee year round and that is why we were so close as a team. For example, I knew Henry's family so well. And even today, we remain close and very good friends. I remember Henry used to get the biggest kick out me when I was on the *Tonight Show* with Johnny Carson over the years. He used to love those spots, especially how I used to talk about all of these fantastic things I didn't do and then make them sound really good. Like it was really special to have two hits in one season. We have been good friends for a long time and as the two of us like to say, 'I can tell you a story about each other, but I can't tell you now!'

"Again, Henry has been a great friend and every time he's in the Milwaukee area he pays a visit to the booth and we just sit back and laugh. It has been a friendship that has stood the test of time. What is sad is that the generation of today and tomorrow never got or will have the opportunity to see someone like Henry Aaron play this game and they don't know what they are missing!"

—Bob Uecker (National Baseball Hall of Fame Ford C. Frick Member, class of 2003)

"Even though I have been a Hall of Famer for over 10 years now it is still overwhelming to me each time we gather with the entire body of Hall of Famers each summer during the Induction Ceremony. And with that, there are still a few of those Hall of Famers that carry with them this incredible sense of respect and Mr. Aaron is one of those players. As each year passes that respect grows more and more. I remember the first time I met Hank Aaron. I was very young and I remember stumbling to say the right words to him. Hank Aaron is just one of those gentlemen whose accomplishments, personality, and integrity seem to rise above most of the people you encounter during your life. One of the biggest impressions he made upon me was how he handled himself while he approached the home run record back in 1974. He never let any of the criticism affect the way he played the game. He also never let any of this impact his teammates. Hank always seems to stay above any of this. Even what has happened most recently in the game with Barry Bonds attempting to break his record and then the negative impacts of how the game changed resulting from that. All of this only helps to elevate Hank's contributions to the game and has made him stand out as even a greater player. His accomplishments are unmatched as well as his contributions both on and off the field. Hank is just one of those great role models. He is

an amazing man and I cherish each opportunity I have when we have that opportunity to get together. Hank is one of those individuals that I always looked up to as a kid and that makes it even more special knowing that we are a part of this unique club known as the Baseball Hall of Fame. Hank Aaron deserves all of the accolades due him."

—Paul Molitor (National Baseball Hall of Fame Member, class of 2004)

Atlanta Braves Archives

"Growing up in Georgia I was a huge Atlanta Braves fan and Hank Aaron meant the world to me. Following Hank Aaron as he chased Babe Ruth's home run record was such an exciting time to witness and to be a fan. I remember the first time we met. It was at Tropicana Field when I was with the Tampa Bay Devil Rays at the end of my career. But now that I am a fellow Hall of Famer it is a special feeling to me whenever we meet. I remember I had the opportunity to spend a lot of time with Hank Aaron at the most recent Hall of Fame Induction Ceremony. I felt like a kid again. I told him what a big fan I was of him and how I grew up in Atlanta and how I followed his career. So, even today, I am a big Hank Aaron fan. He continues to be one of the nicest people you'll ever meet and the funny thing is he doesn't have to be that way given all that he had to put up with and endure, not to mention all of the death threats and the things of that nature. He isn't bitter at all, he is just one of the nicest individuals you'll ever meet."

—Wade Boggs (National Baseball Hall of Fame
Member, class of 2005)

Georgia Sports Hall of Fame

"I played against Hank Aaron and the Milwaukee Brewers when they played us Yankees in the 1957 World Series and they beat us I'm sorry to say! Aaron was a great, great ballplayer and in my opinion was the most legitimate home run hitter of all time. And, I am being very sincere when I say that he was the most legitimate home run champion of all time."

—Jerry Coleman (National Baseball Hall of Fame Ford C. Frick Member, class of 2005)

"Hank Aaron is a player and a name that is synonymous with the game of baseball. Hank is one of the first names I think of when I think about the greatest players that have ever played this game. And, the era that Hank Aaron played in, it wasn't easy for him. I can't even imagine what he must have went through and he was one of the greatest the game has ever seen, and then to do what he did despite all of those obstacles is just incredible. If I were to name five guys on one hand who I consider to be the best, Hank Aaron would be number one or two."

—Ryne Sandberg (National Baseball Hall of Fame Member, class of 2005)

"I came so close to pitching against Hank Aaron when I first came up and broke into the big leagues. It would have been one of the highlights of my career if it did happen. I remember it was spring training in 1975 and Hank Aaron was back with Milwaukee and I was on the mound pitching, trying to make the club. I got the batter out in front of him to end the inning and Hank Aaron was left on deck. Even to this day I wish I would have had the opportunity to face him from a pitching perspective. I guess if I was already on the team back then I would have walked the guy in front of Hank but I was young and I was just trying to make the team so I was just trying to end the inning. But from one Hall of Famer to another, Hank Aaron is still one of these guys when you see him you kind of feel a little uncomfortable around him because he is so special. He is an icon of baseball and in my opinion the greatest player that has ever played this game. And yet, Hank is such a humble person and would probably do anything for you. He is so soft-spoken and a real prince of a guy, but here he is, the best player that has ever played this game. I remember sitting next to him at the Hall of Fame on one occasion and it is a truly humbling experience, and again this is coming from one Hall of Famer to another."

—Bruce Sutter (National Baseball Hall of Fame Member, class of 2006)

"I remember I was about fourteen years old when Hank Aaron was nearing the home run record and that is my best recollection as a fan I have of Hank Aaron growing up. But as I got older everything changed for me and the way I think about Hank Aaron knowing how nice he is. Hank carries himself almost in a royal-like fashion. He walks in a room and the entire dynamics of the room changes and I know others feel the same way about him. And, I've always tried to figure this out to some degree. Is it because he broke the home run record? I know that so many would love to hold that record because it really is the ultimate number in baseball. It is that brass ring everyone aspires for. From that first time we met Hank is everything you want him to be. Hank is such a gentleman and he is so friendly. And at any moment or situation when I have met Hank you come away realizing what a gentlemen and what a great guy he is. Hank is one of the most respectful people you'll ever want to meet. Hank is so respectful to this game. He deserves the utmost respect and carries himself so well. I know from a personal standpoint he has been a part of several experiences that have involved me and as a result has made those experiences even more special and fantastic. In some ways I've had a little more experience with Brooks Robinson over the years because of my affiliation with the Baltimore Orioles but Brooks and Hank are cut from the very same mold. From a player's standpoint I've always been curious how someone with Hank's frame could generate as much bat speed and hit the ball as hard as he did knowing that there were many other ballplayers who possessed a much larger frame than he had. I know many used to compare our swings and mention how similar my swing was to Hank's over the years. I too was a wrist and handsey type of hitter and over the years there were some comparisons that were often made. Hank would look as though he would hit the ball so effortlessly. Over the years the two of us have met several times and many of these chance meetings were at the Baseball Hall of Fame and there is some baseball talk that goes on but I feel it is more like two neighbors who get together and just shoot the breeze. It is just a really nice conversation and it is not like I sit there and we talk about the game and I try and pick his brain for his knowledge, and that is why our discussions are so unique. Hank always lends an ear to what is important in your life at that time.  Hank is a great storyteller but he is also a great listener. Hank Aaron has a genuine curiosity for people and that is what makes him the great person that he is."

—Cal Ripken Jr. (National Baseball Hall of Fame Member, class of 2007)

"Hank Aaron is one of the classiest guys you'll ever meet . . . famous or infamous. There is nothing bad you can ever say about the guy. For me and for so many baseball fans out there we recognize him as a true and great champion and the undisputed Home Run King."

—Richard "Goose" Gossage (National Baseball Hall of Fame Member, class of 2008)

Courtesy of the Pittsburgh Pirates

"I've played with Hank Aaron and I've been on teams which played against him. I think if you talk to every ball player what Hank Aaron means to them you will get a different response from everyone. Fortunately, when I played against Hank Aaron he was still in his prime as a ball player but I was just a youngster . . . new and just trying to understand the game. In 1975, I was playing for the Red Sox and he went on to play with the Milwaukee Brewers and he was such a breath of fresh air for the game. To me, Hank Aaron was the greatest of all-time players that I ever saw play this game. I remember the very first time I played against Hank Aaron I found myself saying to myself, 'I can't believe it . . . I'm playing against Hank Aaron!' a guy that I looked up to so much as I was growing up."

—Jim Rice (National Baseball Hall of Fame Member, class of 2009)

Courtesy of the National Baseball Hall of Fame and Museum

"For me, growing up, Hank Aaron was one of my idols along with Mickey Mantle, Willie Mays, and some of the other stars of that day."

—Andre Dawson (National Baseball Hall of Fame Member, class of 2010)

"For me, growing up, Hank Aaron was one of my idols along with Mickey Mantle, Willie Mays, and some of the other stars of that day. I remember I used to find myself reading as much as I could about them and watch as much footage of their playing days as I could. I did all of this when I was younger because it helped me to be closer to the game. When I reached college I was certainly a Hank Aaron fan because I knew what challenges he faced being an African American to play in this game. Hank Aaron was an impact player knowing that he is often mentioned in the same breath as players like Babe Ruth. I was even more humbled the first time I was able to meet Hank Aaron. He certainly wasn't full of himself or an attention-seeker like he could have been. Hank has always had this smile of confidence and he always seems like he is at peace with himself. You can even tell there is humbleness in his voice when you talk with him. Hank Aaron walks around like he should have a halo over his head. He and his wife are some of the nicest people you'll ever meet. I've met him on several occasions, for example at the Hall of Fame, but I will always remember most the time I really got the opportunity to meet and chat with him. It was during a RBI (Reviving Baseball in Inner Cities) dinner and event. I was just so amazed at how approachable he was and how candid he was with his words. Hank Aaron is just a wonderful, wonderful human being!"

—Andre Dawson (National Baseball Hall of Fame Member, class of 2010)

"I never considered Hank only a home run hitter. I considered him a five-tool player and definitely one of the greatest players of all time. He also was a great defensive player with a great arm. I would consider him one of the top five ballplayers in baseball history."

—Whitey Herzog (National Baseball Hall of Fame Member, class of 2010)

"If you look at the numbers, Hank Aaron may have been one of the greatest players this game has ever seen. Hank had over 3000 hits, 755 home runs, all of those RBIs, he could field, and he could run. I had the honor of facing Hank Aaron at bat when I was only eighteen years old in 1970. It was spring training and I was with the Minnesota Twins and he was with the Atlanta Braves. It was truly an honor to face him, but again he was one of the greatest to ever put on a uniform and a real class[y] human being."

—Bert Blyleven (National Baseball Hall of Fame Member, class of 2011)

Courtesy of the Minnesota Twins

"In my capacity with the Milwaukee Braves as a scout it was very easy to determine that Henry Aaron was the complete package. Henry was outstanding. Henry played the game which also matched his personality. He hustled all of the time; he was never a show boater, and most of all he was a great teammate. He was so enjoyable to watch and then grow as a player, and even though he got better and better his personality and demeanor never changed. Henry played this game so fundamentally well. When he showed up originally in the Braves organization he was a shortstop, a position he held while playing the Negro Leagues for the Indianapolis Clowns. And when he first showed up, very few people knew this but he showed up hitting cross-handed (For a right-handed batter the left hand was above the right hand.) According to Henry, this was a practice that he actually picked up on the sandlots and playgrounds of Mobile while growing up. And I remember all too well the competition there was by several clubs for Henry's service and for him to play for them. I know one of those teams was the New York Giants, and can you imagine a lineup that would have included a Mays and an Aaron? Fortunately, Henry went on to sign with Milwaukee. I give a lot of credit to Syd Pollock, who signed Henry to his first professional contract in 1952 with the Indianapolis Clowns. He helped hold off the Giants and everyone else and then three months later he sold Henry's contract to the Braves.

"Henry's first stop in the Braves organization was in Eau Claire, Wisconsin, where he played shortstop in 1952. I remember in Eau Claire they also tried to make Henry a switch-hitter. I think he even told some people at the time that he felt like he had even more power from the left side of the plate. But he soon stopped hitting left because he accidently hit a ball so hard that it broke the nose of one of his teammates at the time. There was also this issue of the screen that served as the batting cage at the time, but that was the last time Henry ever batted left-handed.

"He then went on to play in Jacksonville, Florida in 1953 as their second baseman. Henry didn't stay too long in the minor leagues because he was such a standout player. Before Henry was promoted to the major leagues, minor league manager Ben Geraghty suggested that he go and play winter ball in 1953 in Puerto Rico. It was there Henry started playing outfield. Geraghty suggested winter ball, figuring that Henry would then have enough experience to move up to the major leagues by spring training in 1954.  So naturally when spring training rolled around, Henry was invited to camp and just like Geraghty had predicted he made the roster. Fortunately for Henry, Bobby Thomson, who was just signed by the Braves, broke his ankle and that left a roster spot for him. Geraghty had such tremendous foresight. Once Henry made the team he got better and better defensively in his new position. This only helped Henry to become that complete ballplayer because he already possessed these tremendous abilities with the bat.

"My greatest memory of Henry was in 1957, when the Braves were fighting their way to the World Series. There was this game we played against the Cardinals and Henry came up with this clutch double, knocking in two runs and eventually helping the team win the game. Sadly, Henry was so underrated, and a lot of that lack of attention came as a result of where he played.

Milwaukee and Atlanta are not known for being big media markets. If Henry would have played in New York baseball fans would have heard the name 'Henry Aaron' many more times. But that didn't match Henry's personality and I think Milwaukee and Atlanta allowed him [to] succeed without all of the scrutiny.

"One of the best stories I can remember about Henry was how he got the jersey number '44'. Henry originally had the number '5' but he always wanted a different number. So, Henry waited until the clubhouse tailor for the Braves went out of town and then he was able to ask the visiting club house manager for a number in the '40s' like his friends on the team, Eddie Mathews and Wes Covington. Mathews had the number '41' and Covington had the number '43'. But that is not the whole story. The visiting clubhouse manager got into some hot water because apparently it was a rule back then by Major League Baseball not to issue any changes to players' numbers at the time. For Henry's sake he got his number changed and the '44' stuck around for the rest of his career!"

—Roland Hemond (National Baseball Hall of Fame Member Buck O'Neil Lifetime Achievement Award, class of 2011)

"Hank Aaron was a magnificent ballplayer. He's known for his home runs but in every other way he did everything he could to help his team win. Hank Aaron could hit, he could run the bases, and he could field his position . . . Hank Aaron could do it all!"

—Tim McCarver (National Baseball Hall of Fame Ford C. Frick Member, class of 2012)

"I didn't play against Hank Aaron when he was playing this game, but I certainly met him on many occasions, especially every time I broadcasted a game that he played in. I'm not the last word on the subject, but Hank Aaron always let his bat do the talking for him . . . he must have had this talking bat that always knew what to do. Hank is and will always be one of my favorite guys. I think Hank Aaron has been so underrated over the years. Hank was such a great all-around ballplayer, but everyone just thinks about the home runs he hit. Hank was a strong and quiet type that did the job he was paid to do and he did it so well and he ended up in the Hall of Fame and deservingly so. I am and I will always be a big Hank Aaron fan."

—Joe Garagiola (National Baseball Hall of Fame Member Buck O'Neil Lifetime Achievement Award, class of 2014)

Atlanta Braves Archives

"My first experience with Hank Aaron was in August 1971. I was traded to the Braves so I had the opportunity to spend the last six to seven weeks that season as his teammate. I may have only gotten seven at-bats for the team, but I got to see Hank in all of his playing glory. Hank was still able to command all of the respect he deserved. I don't care what sport you play; the great ones always have this sense of aura. And knowing Hank the way I do now and knowing the kind heart he has makes it even more special to talk about him now. I have two experiences from my playing days concerning Hank Aaron, besides his tremendous body of work and observing his greatness. But I remember being on the bench and having other players on the team say to me, 'Okay, Hank's up so let's get our bets down.' The bet was how many times in a row would Hank hit the ball hard. So, never being exposed to the bet before I said, 'I say nine in a row!' Then everyone started to laugh at me. They all knew I was way off. Apparently, the winning bet was generally about 14 or 15 in a row. In this particular situation the winning bet was 17 or 18 consecutive times in a row Hank hit the ball well and right off of the barrel. But, to be fair, I thought initially he should hit well in one, two, and maybe three games in a row. That is how I came up with the number nine for the bet. But again, they all laughed at me like I was an idiot and I was. I think the closest bet even to me was thirteen. It was ridiculous to think about it that way but that is all Hank ever seemed to do, snap those wrists and he would always hit the ball hard. Hank Aaron represents the best of what fans like to believe what the great hitters and the great pitchers are all about; that there is true greatness in every performance. I really hope that character translates beyond the field, and in

Hank's case it does. Meaning if you meet them on the street that they would be the person you feel good about meeting and who are never arrogant. Hank is one of those players you feel better about after you meet him, even to this day. Hank does this great job of representing himself, his family, the organization, and major league baseball. Whenever I meet Hank he makes the experience and situation that much better because of who he is. And, when he isn't there the experience and situation is not as special. I remember when I played on his team in 1971 and we started to talk about our careers, and my career at the time was nothing to write home about, but it was so special and neat when Hank started to recall his career and recap his experiences against let's say the Dodgers. It was great hearing his stories about these incredible battles he had against the Dodgers and against Koufax and Drysdale during a truly golden age of baseball."

—Tony LaRussa (National Baseball Hall of Fame Member, class of 2014)

"I grew up my whole life knowing that Hank Aaron was the Home Run King. So, when you think of home runs you think of Hank Aaron and Babe Ruth. I always knew this to be a special thing. To me Hank Aaron is an extremely nice man and is very humble all of the times I would encounter him. On the occasion or two I did get the opportunity to speak with him during my Atlanta Braves playing days, it always seemed like it was on a plane going from this place or that city and I would have the chance to sit next to him. Hank Aaron to me has always been one of those impact players and for me one of the greatest players that this game has ever seen. He is certainly at the top of the list. I remember I used to park off of 755 Hank Aaron Way,

the address of the Atlanta Braves Stadium, every day, so how could you not think about him each day you came to the ballpark? He was a part of my daily routine. I remember my coolest time pitching to anyone was when I had the opportunity to face Pete Rose when he was a player-manager. But, if I had a bucket list of players I wish I could have faced, Hank Aaron would have definitely been on that list."

—Greg Maddux (National Baseball Hall of Fame Member, class of 2014)

"Henry Aaron is total class and I am proud to say that I've known him since I was a teenager. Not to mention he is a good friend.  For my sake, I was able to witness Henry in his prime. I remember when we first met he was a skinny kid and he had these incredibly quick wrists. I watched him play and it was like watching pure elegance. Henry always seemed like he glided around the field and the way he played the game. One of the first memories I have of Henry was in 1956. I took my first plane ride to Milwaukee to spend some time with my brother who was playing for the Braves at that time. I remember being at one of the games and I was sitting on the third base side of the field behind the visitor's dugout in Milwaukee. And, what really caught my attention was when Henry came up to bat and his back was to me. It was a day game and Henry got this pitch that was literally behind and past him and yet, because he was so quick with those wrists, he hit that ball for a home run over the right field fence. Again, that really caught my attention and made me realize at a very young age how really good this guy (Henry) was. People over the years wanted to see Henry hit the long ball and I am sure they were not disappointed, but I am convinced he could pretty much will the ball to do whatever he wanted. Henry became a pull hitter because of what the fans wanted him to become. He also became a pull hitter because he was able to do it but as far as purity there really wasn't any place safe in that ballpark that Henry wasn't dangerous. For years I hit behind Henry in the lineup and I used to get the biggest kick out of these young pitchers who tried to pitch Henry on the inside of the plate, thinking they could sneak it by him and get him out. More times than I could count the ball usually found its way to the seats somewhere up and over the fence. No matter how fast they tried to throw it he'd usually hit it hard. No matter if their intentions were to move him back or get him to swing he would make them pay and again that ball would generally find its way to the seats. I've always admired Henry and I know he was always a special player. He never showed any weaknesses. Henry could do it all. I do remember one pitcher who gave Henry fits at the plate. It was Curt Simmons and he used to throw Henry this slow curve. It was actually comical watching him hit against Simmons. Henry would swing so hard and the ball would go about ten feet in the air. It was the funniest thing in the world. Simmons would make him swing and miss so much. I do remember on one occasion Henry trying to get the best of Simmons one day at old Busch Stadium. Simmons threw him one of those slow curves and Henry ran up before it could drop and he hit the ball on the roof for a home run but it was the catcher for the Cardinals, who called attention to the umpire that Henry's left foot was out of the batter's box and then he called him out. Henry didn't like it! I know if I ever had a bucket list of players I wish I could have coached Henry would certainly be on that list because of the type of player he was. He was one of those players that literally managed themselves. I was fortunate to coach several of these types of players over the years especially when I was with the Yankees organization, who again had the ability to coach themselves. Henry was such a quiet leader. He used to kid around a lot with Eddie Mathews in the clubhouse but for the most part he was anonymous. Henry never sought the attention or the limelight.

"The one thing they never gave Henry enough credit for was how efficient a base stealer he was. He never stole bases for any totals; he stole bases for the situation. For example, there would be situations late in the game when Henry would get on base and he would get you that extra base when you needed it. I remember he would be on first base and I would be hitting behind him and then I'd get the bunt sign to move him over, and I wasn't a good bunter. So, I would usually end up bunting the ball right back to the pitcher and in most cases it should have been a play when the pitcher could get the lead runner going to second. But, because Henry was so good at baserunning and would get such an incredible jump on the ball they weren't able to throw him out at second and would concentrate on me at first. So, Henry would end up making me look good because it allowed me to get the sacrifice down. Then, I remember playing this game against the Cubs and Henry was on first and I was hitting. And, as a player you sometimes take a quick peek around the field while you are batting. On this occasion, I peeked down at first to get a look at Henry and hopefully give him a chance to steal a base. I was facing their pitcher Chuck Hartenstein. I never faced him before and he got two quick strikes on me. So again, I took a peek at Henry thinking that if [he] got caught on the next pitch and I got a ball then I would have another chance to bat with a clean slate the next inning. And, he did. Henry was stealing second and in just that moment I got clocked in the face with the next pitch. I learned a valuable lesson that night to keep my eye on the pitch! But again, Henry was a remarkable base runner and base stealer. He was a great team player and I am proud to call him a good friend."

—Joe Torre (National Baseball Hall of Fame Member, class of 2014)

Left to Right: Joe Torre, Felipe Alou, Mack Jones, Hank Aaron

"Hank Aaron is one of those icons of the game that becomes bigger and bigger the more years that go by. As the years pass, we appreciate the efforts he put forth in the way he did it and during that moment in history. He was always a perfect gentleman to me when I was coming up. I never imagined being a part of an organization which Hank Aaron called home for so long. It was pretty cool. I've always said, 'Hank Aaron was the greatest home run hitter of all time' and that is something you didn't appreciate as much when he was doing it as it is today. Hank Aaron will always be someone special to me!"

—John Smoltz (National Baseball Hall of Fame Member, class of 2015)

# Former Players and Teammates

Atlanta Braves Archives

"According to a quote by Hank Aaron I read, I apparently was one of the toughest pitchers he ever faced. I think this was the case because later in my career I began throwing this slow curveball. I was a left-handed pitcher who had this herky-jerky motion and I honestly think I threw Hank Aaron off his game. I'd throw him mostly this slow curve. I developed this pitch for players like Hank to get them out of their swing. But you don't face Hank Aaron as much as I did without him getting the better hand on me. Hank certainly hit his share of home runs off of me. I'm not sure how many home runs he hit, but I do remember this one home run he hit off of me in St. Louis when I was with the Cardinals. It was off of my fastball. Did that ball ever go far! It was on fire and from that point on I said to myself, 'I'm not going to let him (Hank Aaron) beat me again off of my fastball.' So, from that point on, I began to throw Hank Aaron nothing but my slow curve. Then there was this game in St. Louis, later in my career, when I faced Hank and he knew he was going to get one of those slow curveballs and he decided to step up and out of the batter's box and get to the pitch before it dropped. Well, it worked, Hank hit this home run so far and onto the short porch and roof of St. Louis' stadium, but the umpire saw what he did and called him out because he caught him stepping out of the box. So, what appeared to be a two-run home run ended up being the third out of the inning and I guess Hank had one less home run in his great career. Hank Aaron was one of the greatest hitters I ever faced and he forced me to change the way I was pitching. But, anyway, I think Hank might have had a little trouble hitting off of me too."

—Curt Simmons (Major League pitcher 1949–1958; played for the Philadelphia Phillies, St. Louis Cardinals, Chicago Cubs, and California Angels)

Georgia Sports Hall of Fame

"Well, I remember pitching two shutout games against Milwaukee the year they won the World Championship. I pitched a two-hit shutout against them and a 12-inning nothing-nothing matchup against them that was eventually rained out. But, more importantly I remember also being pretty lucky because I think in all the times I faced Hank Aaron I only gave up two home runs to him. When I faced Hank Aaron he was in his prime, and hell he could hit. I never saw in all my days someone as spectacular as him. Hank Aaron was an unbelievable hitter. Hank was one of the best of all time and I've seen them all. No doubt about it. I faced the likes of Stan Musial, Duke Snider, Del Ennis, Eddie Mathews, Roy Campanella—just to name a few—and he was the best at what he did. I know there is always that debate as to who was the best and it is hard to sometimes single it out as to who was the best but in my book, having faced him as many times as I did, it was Hank Aaron."

—Bob Miller (Major League pitcher 1949–1958;
played for the Philadelphia Phillies)

"First of all, Hank Aaron is a dear friend of mine. He is a friend of mine who also happened to be an opponent of mine. We were friends, but sometimes I had to pitch against him and on occasion I would get him out and sometimes he used to beat my brains out with the way he hit off of me. But, after the game we would have fun together and laugh about the good times and it wasn't always about baseball. I would like to share with you a letter I received a few years ago from Henry Aaron . . .

*Congratulations Don on reaching 85 years old but I have to admit it that it is hard to believe. In my head, you will forever be that young and veteran pitcher who was so tough on the field and so helpful off the field. On the mound Don Newcombe was as good as they get. He broke in the game during a time when black players had to be more than good enough. They had to excel in order to make a big league roster. You could be as dominant and crafty as anyone in the game. When it came to sheer competitiveness I never faced anyone fiercer. But, what meant the most to me was the side of you that only a few of us saw. I remember how you reached out to me and other black players who were trying to establish themselves as major leaguers. You know how high the odds were and how the deck was stacked against us and how much we had to deal with, that is because you were dealing with it too. When the Dodgers and Braves headed north during spring training and we played exhibition games we played in cities where segregation was still the law. So the blacks from both teams would stay in the same hotel and eat in the same diners. For me, those times were an education like none other. You and Jackie and Campy (Roy Campanella) taught me to stay focused and not get distracted. You were living and breathing role models of how to play the game and how to carry yourself as a man. To me, you three were mentors and friends who had more influence on my early career than any coach or teammate. So, I am honored to say Happy Birthday and thanks to a man whose courage and friendship provided a guiding light to the most critical time of my life. And, I am sure glad I don't have to stand against you tonight. Happy Birthday and many more.*

*—Hank Aaron*

"What more can be said? About a man and what he feels about me and how he felt about me when he and I were just young kids trying to play this game and how we were all after the same goal . . . of how to play major league baseball and how we had to fight against those who didn't want to see that happen. I was lucky enough to be on the same team as Jackie and Roy. There were two of the greatest teachers you could have ever been exposed to. I went on and had what I believe is a fine career and I had many matchups against Hank Aaron over the years. When I got a chance to play against him I never threw at Hank Aaron intentionally. I didn't care how many home runs he hit against me, and he hit many. I never knocked him down and Hank knew that and that is why we were such great friends after the game. We have been friends since he broke into the game with the Braves and I came into the game with the Dodgers and we are still friends.

"Hank was the most talented player I ever saw play this game. I know there have been a lot of comparisons over the years as to who was the greatest player. But for me as a pitcher, Hank was the toughest out I ever faced. I remember this one game in 1955, against the Braves in Milwaukee. Hank came up the first time at bat and got a single off of me. The next time up he hit a home run. The next time up he slid into second with a double. And I remember walking near the base and I called over to Hank and said kiddingly, 'Mr. Aaron, next time you come up I'm going to throw my shoe at you. See how far you could hit that one!' Those who happened to hear my statement took it all out of context and thought I was saying something negatively to Hank. It even appeared in the

newspaper the next day reflecting that same negative tone. I remember after the game we got together and laughed about it.

"I am so glad I had this opportunity to talk about my great friend Hank Aaron. I'm eighty-eight years old now and I don't remember everything but I certainly remember my friend Hank Aaron. And, because of the person Hank is and all of his greatness that comes with him I am so proud of what he has done throughout his lifetime and career. I guess you can say I am a proud member of the Hank Aaron Fan Club!"

—Don Newcombe (Major League pitcher 1949–1960; played for the Brooklyn Dodgers, Los Angeles Dodgers, Cincinnati Redlegs, Cincinnati Reds, and Cleveland Indians)

"If it wasn't for me, Henry Aaron would have only hit 754 home runs! I'm proud to say Henry only hit one home run off of me over the years. And, what was funny about that is he hit the home run off of me in my final year in the big leagues while I was in Montreal for the Expos in 1969. It was a great way for him to say 'goodbye and good luck' I suppose. But in all seriousness, Henry Aaron was one of the best players that has ever played this game and too many people have forgotten how well-rounded he was. For example, Henry Aaron was also a great outfielder. He never made a lot of mistakes. He could run the bases and do everything right as a player. Henry Aaron was one of the better ones I faced and I have always had tremendous respect for him. I will also always remember the quote he said about me, 'When Face came into the ballgame it usually meant the game was all over.' And when Henry Aaron says that about you it can make you feel really good inside and that you know you did everything you could as a player."

—Elroy Face (Major League pitcher 1953–1969; played for the Pittsburgh Pirates, Detroit Tigers, and Montreal Expos)

"I played against Hank Aaron for many years and I've seen him hit many of his home runs. Hank was a truly remarkable player but the thing that always impressed me the most about him was how great an all-around hitter he was. I'm convinced if he wasn't hitting home runs Hank would have led the league seven, eight, or even nine times in hitting if he wanted to hit for high average. But when the home runs started coming then the fans wanted to see him hit nothing but home runs and from that point on Henry became more of a pull hitter. Hank used to use the entire field when he started playing. He was a great hitter early on and he became a greater hitter when he hit the home runs. Of course, there is an old saying in baseball that goes like this, 'Players who hit home runs drive Cadillacs and those players who hit singles drive Fords!' But Hank was such a complete ballplayer. He was also a great right fielder. He had this great arm and he was also this great baserunner. There was nothing Henry couldn't do.

"Being around as long as I have been around this game you get to like some players because of the way they played the game, their style you may want to call it, and Hank was one of these players to me. Hank Aaron was an amazing ballplayer and I miss seeing him play and what is sad is that this generation out there and those generations still to come have completely missed this great player too."

—Don Zimmer (Major League infielder, manager, and coach 1954–2014; played for the Brooklyn Dodgers and Washington Senators)

Atlanta Braves Archives

"I have known Hank Aaron for years. What Hank Aaron has done for this game is unbelievable. I have always marveled at the player Hank was. Hank will always be a part of baseball history and is just so far up there in terms of his accomplishments on and off the field. I can tell you this: Hank Aaron is a very smart man because he once hired me to be his pitching coach in the minor leagues for the Braves! It's something I even get to tell my great-grandchildren, that I was hired by Hank Aaron, and then they said 'Poppy…who is Hank Aaron?' and then I get the opportunity to tell them the stories of this great man. Sometimes, I worry because his accomplishments are so silent around the game because of Hank's quiet demeanor and because he wasn't flashy. He just always got the job done. Yet, he faced as many problems as Jackie and many of the early black ballplayers. Hank was just one of those guys you are glad you faced during your career and now my great-grandchildren say how 'cool' Hank Aaron is."

—Jim "Mudcat" Grant (Major League pitcher 1958–1971; played for the Cleveland Indians, Minnesota Twins, Los Angeles Dodgers, Montreal Expos, St. Louis Cardinals, Oakland Athletes, and Pittsburgh Pirates)

"I faced Hank Aaron many times. Actually, Hank Aaron was always one of the toughest outs for me during my pitching days. Hank was a great ballplayer similar to the likes of Stan Musial and Willie Mays. Hank was a great guy and very unassuming, but he was a true superstar. I remember at one point during my pitching days he had this streak of going 8 for 8 against me and not to mention a few walks thrown in there as well. But then one day he hit this ground ball off of me down the first base side. I went to cover first base and I remember saying to myself, 'I'm finally going to get this SOB out.' Then I fittingly pulled my hamstring. I guess it was like 'an eye for an eye.' But in all my years I have had the greatest respect for Hank Aaron from a pitcher's perspective because he was one of the toughest outs and competitors this game has ever seen."

—Ron Perranoski (Major League pitcher and coach 1961–1973; played for the Los Angeles Dodgers, Minnesota Twins, Detroit Tigers, California Angels. Coach for the Los Angeles Dodgers from 1981–1994 and San Francisco Giants 1997–1999)

"I did face Hank Aaron on several occasions and he was as good as they all said he was. Hank had these powerful wrists which allowed him to wait as long as possible to hit the ball and when he did connect and hit that ball there always seemed to be a lot of enthusiasm with that ball because it generally meant it left the ballpark pretty fast. I remember he hit his share of home runs off of me. In fact, he hit two home runs in one game off of me. Hank was one of those players that you could not make any mistakes when it came to pitching to him and even when you did throw a good pitch at him he'd still hit the ball hard off of you. Hank Aaron was an awesome hitter and being a pitcher it was very difficult to pitch well to him because he had very little if any weaknesses. Even my best wasn't always the best for him!"

—Dave Giusti (Major League pitcher 1962–1977; played for the Houston Colt .45s, Houston Astros, St. Louis Cardinals, Pittsburgh Pirates, Oakland Athletics, and Chicago Cubs)

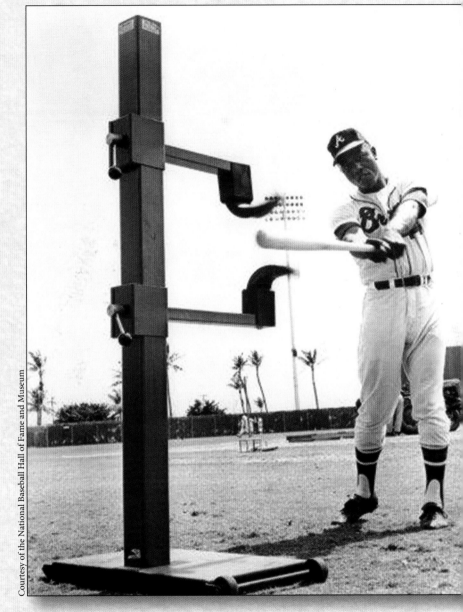

"Hank Aaron was a quiet man and a super friend and a great teammate. Hank Aaron was a perfect gentleman and is the greatest home run hitter this game has ever witnessed and to me one of the greatest ballplayers that has ever played this game."

—Denny McLain (Major League pitcher 1963–1972; played for the Detroit Tigers, Washington Senators, Oakland Athletics, and Atlanta Braves)

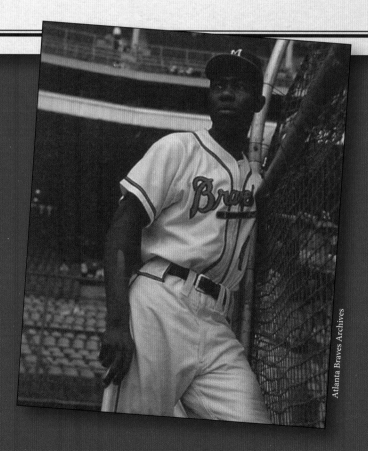

*Atlanta Braves Archives*

"I know I gave up my share of home runs, I believe six from what I remember, to Hank Aaron over the years, so I feel in some way like I helped contribute to his record in a small way! It may have only been 749 home runs without me. As a young pitcher I too suffered my lumps; Hank Aaron, Willie McCovey, and Willie Mays all got the best of me at one point or another. But, I guess it was all part of the learning process for a young pitcher and if you wanted to pitch in the big leagues. Hank Aaron was always a little different in my book. He was like Rod Carew with a lot more power. As a pitcher against players like that you start asking yourself, 'What can I possibly do to get this guy out?' Players like Hank Aaron and Rod Carew never seemed fooled. They always seemed to know what pitch you were going to throw. They seemed to always know if the pitch would be in the strike zone or not and if they could hit it or not. Hank was so incredibly tough to get out. What amazed me as a pitcher it never seemed like any of his home runs were monster or massive shots or by tape measure standards. They always appeared to be line drives that left the ballpark so quickly. It was like he was always hitting with a two iron. Hank Aaron just never seemed to miss. If you made a mistake as a pitcher you paid for it . . . you absolutely paid for it!"

—Rick Wise (Major League pitcher 1964–1982; played for the Philadelphia Phillies, St. Louis Cardinals, Boston Red Sox, Cleveland Indians, and San Diego Padres)

"Hank Aaron was always an extremely tough out. That goes without saying. I was a sinkerball pitcher and I didn't like to come in on batters too often, especially guys as good as Hank Aaron. I'd pitch him low and away and he still got to me a few times more then I liked. As a pitcher you would often think to yourself, 'What am I going to do with him?' My best wasn't always good enough for Hank Aaron. He was tough and you couldn't fool him. Hank Aaron was a great player!"

—Darold Knowles (Major League pitcher and coach 1965–1980; played for the Baltimore Orioles, Philadelphia Phillies, Washington Senators, Oakland Athletes, Chicago Cubs, Texas Rangers, Montreal Expos, and St. Louis Cardinals)

Atlanta Braves Archives

"I had the opportunity to face Hank Aaron on several occasions. The time I remember the most was when my manager at the time, Danny Ozark with the Philadelphia Phillies, had me walk Darrell Evans three different times to get to Hank Aaron. That was funny to me and I really wanted to ask him, 'Hey Danny! Don't you think we are playing with fire here?' Because sooner or later Hank Aaron was going to make us pay for that. I guess Danny never heard of the expression 'Three times the charm.' Amazingly enough I got Hank Aaron out on all three occasions and I guess Danny then looked like a genius. I remember Hank Aaron was so quick, especially on pitches on the inside part of the plate; and being the sinker pitcher I would throw the ball and even though I was pretty lucky when I faced Hank I always felt like I was playing with fire."

—Gene Garber (Major League pitcher 1969–1988; played for the Pittsburgh Pirates, Kansas City Royals, Philadelphia Phillies, and Atlanta Braves)

"I had a close personal relationship with Hank and even today he is the type of person that I can still call and get advice. Hank has always been so gracious. As for his ability as a player, Hank was such a fierce competitor and as great as he was I don't believe he ever got the recognition he deserved. And, much of that was also because of Hank's personality. He was never showy or flamboyant. Despite all of the controversy I still consider him the Home Run King and I feel strongly about that. But you will never find Hank Aaron speaking negatively about the record or about the events that have occurred more recently with the steroids and such use. It is a very difficult game, baseball, and for Hank to put up the numbers Hank did and then doing it the right way really lets you know a little bit of how great he really was when he played this game. Hank is so respected by all players and to know him on a personal basis is really special to me. Hank had endured so much during a very difficult timeframe. I can't imagine chasing the record he did and then to get the hate mail and then to face those who spoke so passionately because they didn't want to see you break this record is why so many of us love, respect, and honor him so much, not just on the baseball field but on a personal level."

—Gary Matthews (Major League outfielder 1972–1987; played for the San Francisco Giants, Philadelphia Phillies, Atlanta Braves, Chicago Cubs, and Seattle Mariners)

"I faced Hank Aaron on several occasions. Hank was at the end of his career when I came along. I am only one of two pitchers to give up a home run to both Hank Aaron and Barry Bonds. I remember Hank Aaron as very selective when it came to being a hitter. He didn't seem to ever chase a ball out of the strike zone. And because he never chased bad pitches he was very patient waiting for that certain pitch that he could hit. Barry Bonds was also very patient as well. He was probably more willing to take the walk if he didn't get a pitch he liked. And, Barry was such a great hitter too. They both had tremendous bat speed; Hank had a bit longer swing as opposed to Barry, who had this quick, short swing."

—Rick Reuschel (Major League pitcher 1972–1991; played for the Chicago Cubs, New York Yankees, Pittsburgh Pirates, and San Francisco Giants)

Courtesy of the National Baseball Hall of Fame and Museum

"When I faced Hank Aaron I was just a young pup in one of my first seasons trying to break into the game and I know Hank Aaron hadn't lost a step even though he was more at the tail end or twilight of his career. Hank Aaron was an incredible ballplayer who had this amazing career when I first faced him. I was in some ways the perfect pitcher for him. I was a fastball pitcher and Hank was a great fastball hitter. I used to like to come inside to challenge the hitters, but when you're a hitter like Hank Aaron you don't mind a ball on the inside part of the plate. So, as you might predict, Hank Aaron was able to get those incredibly quick hands going, generate the bat speed that he did, and was able to take the ball out of the park. Someone told me recently that I was only one of two pitchers to give up a home run to Hank Aaron and to Barry Bonds, a feat I guess I can be pretty proud of! Barry, of course, came at you from the other side of the plate. He too had this incredible bat speed and was able to generate so much power. When you make mistakes to hitters like Hank and Barry they are going to make you pay for it. You might get away with it on some occasions but most of the time you don't. I guess the shocking thing would have been if they didn't hit a home run off of me."

—Frank Tanana (Major League pitcher 1973–1993 played for the California Angels, Boston Red Sox, Texas Rangers, Detroit Tigers, New York Mets, and New York Yankees)

"I remember the day when Hank Aaron broke Babe Ruth's home run record like it was yesterday. I remember him hitting that home run. I remember when I saw it and what I was thinking knowing that hit was such an important milestone and how encouraging it was for so many black ballplayers who were playing this game or were struggling and new to the game at that particular time. Hank Aaron was such an important player and figure, not to mention what a great role model he was for the game when he played and even today."

—Ron Leflore (Major League outfielder 1974–1982; played for the Detroit Tigers, Montreal Expos, and Chicago White Sox)

"My first big league spring training was in 1973. I was nineteen years old and we were in Fort Lauderdale, Florida and I was facing the Atlanta Braves during the fourth, fifth, and sixth innings. And, I remember when Hank Aaron first came up to the plate to bat and I was on the mound, I remember saying to myself, 'Wow! That is Hank Aaron. I have a ball, I just wish I had a pen for him to sign it!' And then I said, 'Wait! I'm facing Hank Aaron, now how am I going to get him out?' That was the big question. Then a few years later I had my first big league call-up in late September, 1976, with the Baltimore Orioles and we were facing the Milwaukee Brewers that last season series. It was Hank Aaron's last season in the big leagues because everyone knew he was going to retire. It was the last game of the series and I ended up facing Hank once again. But this time, being a recent call-up and thinking I am all that, I said to myself, 'Hey, I can get this guy out.' The next thing I know he was doubling down the line. But, I did get my wish; later that day and after the game, he signed a baseball for me and signed it, 'To Scott from Hank Aaron.' I still have that ball and it will always be special to me. Hank Aaron will always be one of the greats of the game and he will definitely be a part of my history."

—Scott McGregor (Major League pitcher and coach 1976–1988; played for the Baltimore Orioles)

"I signed with the Atlanta Braves in 1974 and I got my first call-up two years later. So, I just missed playing directly with Hank Aaron because by 1976 he went back to Milwaukee. Hank did hold positions with the Braves organization during my playing days there. We would always seem to miss a direct connection, but I always knew Hank was there. And, I can only say good things about him. I have such great admiration for him. I still can't figure out how he hit all of those home runs. Hank was just this model of consistency. It is absolutely mind-boggling to do what he did. For example, I'm not bragging but I was able to hit my share of home runs over my career. But, I still only hit 398 home runs and even if I made it to the 400 home run plateau I still would be 355 home runs short of reaching Hank. I can't just grasp what that must have been like. It is amazing to think about that consistency and the number of years he continued to put up the numbers he did. And, you can't diminish the conditions he went through because of the racial issues and especially when he was approaching Babe Ruth's home run record. I'm sure there must have been a love fest that was going on in baseball with Hank Aaron on the outside, but I can't imagine the pain he must have been experiencing on the inside. Baseball is hard enough to play and to play it well is even tougher. All you want to do as a ballplayer is just to do your job but then to handle what Hank had to endure beginning in the minor leagues and then up in the major leagues and all of that discrimination. Based on that, I'm not sure how he was able to perform at the level he did as a player. So often in the course of human history we see the right man at the right time. And, we don't remember when it's not the right person because the whole thing just falls apart. But Hank Aaron was the right man at the right time and probably he was the only man that could handle all that he did. For the rest of us, if we go 0-4 in a game and someone writes something negatively about us in the newspaper the next day it could mess you up for a week. But that wasn't the case for Hank Aaron. He had so much strength and character not to break. Hank Aaron was remarkable and his numbers prove that. You know there are some guys who put up good numbers but they still are few and far between. For example, there is only one DiMaggio, or Mantle, or Ted Williams, or Pete Rose, and these players were all able to put up amazing numbers but they did it in a racial climate that was friendly to them and then there was Hank Aaron, who was exposed to a climate that wasn't always so friendly. And, then to pursue the record he did is a remarkable achievement."

—Dale Murphy (Major League outfielder 1976–1993; played for the Atlanta Braves, Philadelphia Phillies, and Colorado Rockies)

Courtesy of the National Baseball Hall of Fame and Museum

"I was always so impressed how powerful of a man Hank Aaron was and he always seemed to have the quickest wrists of anybody I ever witnessed. I remember catching against Hank in my first year of baseball and [it] was his last year in the big leagues. I was very young, but I was in constant amazement being in a situation to catch against him and even to this day it is one of the highlights of my career. There were always certain guys who were your favorites because you love this game so much. Hank Aaron was one of these players you idolized. Hank was always in that group of players, for me, who consistently made the roster as to who were your favorite players year in and year out."

—John Wathan (Major League catcher and manager 1976–1985; and 1987–1992 played for and managed the Kansas Royals and California Angels)

"Hank Aaron was a great ballplayer. Hank was incredibly consistent and what amazed me was given all of those home runs he never hit more than 50 home runs in a single season. Hank was never given enough credit for all of those hits he accumulated and all of those RBIs. Most people don't think about his production and that part of the game when it came to Hank Aaron. Once again, Hank Aaron was a great ballplayer and he did it all during a very difficult timeframe when it came to race relations and that also shows to me what kind of man Hank Aaron was and how strong his character was knowing that he kept a lot of that away from his teammates and didn't let it affect his game. Given all of that, this is why Hank Aaron is so special to me."

—Harold Baines (Major League outfielder, designated hitter, and coach 1981–1992; played for the Chicago White Sox, Texas Rangers, Oakland Athletes, Baltimore Orioles, and Cleveland Indians)

"When you think about the greats of the game you think of Hank Aaron and players like him who helped pave the groundwork for the modern-day players of today. Hank Aaron was one of those players that helped with this transition. It's true Jackie Robinson really changed the game, but it was players like Hank Aaron who helped solidify the game for everyone. Guys I faced like Ozzie Smith, Reggie Jackson, and Dusty Baker experienced a lot of the racial issues Hank Aaron and those early guys did, but at least they had those players like Hank and Jackie to turn to. Just like the players of today can turn to the players that I faced during my playing days as inspiration. There were certain players who were always your favorite, because of the way they played the game, and Hank Aaron was one of those players I idolized."

—Jay Howell (Major League pitcher 1980–1994; played for the Cincinnati Reds, Chicago Cubs, New York Yankees, Oakland Athletes, Los Angeles Dodgers, Atlanta Braves, and Texas Rangers)

"Hank Aaron did everything well. He ran the bases well, he had this incredible arm, and of course he could hit, and he could hit for power, but most of all he was a smart player, and he didn't make a lot of mistakes. He did what he had to do on an everyday basis and helped his team win ball games. Hank Aaron was such a complete ballplayer!"

—Jesse Barfield (Major League outfielder 1981–1992; played for the Toronto Blue Jays and New York Yankees)

"Hank Aaron was always my favorite ballplayer growing up. Everyone has players they liked watching but then as a kid you have your all-time favorite and for me that was Hank Aaron. And, he was my favorite for many reasons; there was the home run record and the chase leading up to it, and all of the other records, but most importantly because for me Hank Aaron is this game's greatest ambassador. And, what better person for Major League Baseball to have as their ambassador but Hank Aaron, for what he did as a player and after he retired."

—Dmitri Young (Major League first baseman, outfielder, and designated hitter 1996–2008; played for the St. Louis Cardinals, Cincinnati Reds, Detroit Tigers, and Washington Nationals)

# Atlanta Braves Teammates and that Magical 1974 Season

Courtesy of the Georgia Sports Hall of Fame

"I was offered a bunch of college scholarships to play baseball. I remember they would fly my mom and me out to the different schools. I had a choice to make because I was also drafted by the Atlanta Braves in 1967 out of my high school near Sacramento, California. That is when I first met

Hank. He assured my mother that he would treat me like his own son and look after me. And, that was enough of an assurance to my mother. It was pretty special. So, my mom let me sign with the Atlanta Braves after Hank spoke with her. From that point on, Ralph (Garr) and I were always around Hank. That was even prior to us making it to the big leagues. Hank would take us around and he wouldn't even let us pay for anything. Hank would tell us to go to bed. He would tell us to go to church. He was like a big brother but he was Hank Aaron. But, that is what he told my mom, that he would look after me. We were with Hank every day and it was special because I was just this nineteen-year-old kid and hanging out with Hank Aaron was pretty cool. Hank was so disciplined, confident, and humble. He never talked about the negative. Hank was a mentor, our friend, and our big brother. We would always go to talk to Hank about everything. The worst day for us was opening day 1975 when Hank went

on to play for the Milwaukee Brewers and left the Braves organization. We were all alone and naked in the woods, as they say. The next year was the same for us. But you have to understand, Hank was the guy who held it all together for the whole Braves team, and for a time he held it all together for the country. Hank had the weight of the world on his shoulders. I remember the only time Hank felt down was when he was going through his divorce. Hank was hurting bad because he didn't have his family and kids around and he had to live downtown. But, then when he met Billye everything turned around. I remember he had me and Ralph meet Billye one day. And, I said to Hank kiddingly, 'You don't need my approval or permission!'

"Hank taught us everything; He even taught us when we should eat our meals so this way we would be at our strongest at game time. Hank was such a professional. Hank introduced us to everyone from civic leaders, to politicians, to entertainers. We met everyone because of Hank Aaron. I always considered Hank in the same category as my father. And Hank did all of this during a very difficult and volatile timeframe for our country. Anyone who was not around during that time must have a difficult time trying to understand the feelings of that era. All of the racial concerns, the Vietnam War, the assassinations that had occurred, it was such a different and difficult timeframe. But Hank was actually what we needed. The world needed a hero and they got one. Sadly, many didn't appreciate him until later. Hank was a lot like Muhammad Ali. Not because of how flashy he was but because their efforts were not appreciated until years later. Ralph and I were so lucky to be with him every day. We couldn't get any more inner-circled than we were. We all knew about the threats and the hate mail. I remember on an occasion or two I watched Hank read the letter and then he would throw it to the ground of the clubhouse. I'd pick it up and read them. I read the hate and I never understood it. But I also witnessed how Hank would deal with it and things like that and I know it helped me as I grew as a man and as a player. I have a thousand and one stories about Hank but recently I think this one will help sum it up as to what type of man Hank Aaron is and how he is now perceived. I remember we were playing in Atlanta a few seasons back when I was managing the Reds. I would tell my players all about Hank and one day while there Hank came to visit me in my manager's office. Players like Joey Votto and Jay Bruce saw Hank in there and they knocked on the door and asked me to introduce them. I did and all they wanted to do is just meet and talk with Hank and they did. They were like two little kids."

—Dusty Baker (Major League second baseman and World Series Manager 1968–1986; played for the Atlanta Braves, Los Angeles Dodgers, San Francisco Giants, and Oakland Athletics. Managed from 1993–2013 for the San Francisco Giants, Chicago Cubs, and Cincinnati Reds.)

"I was probably one of the few pitchers in the game that gave up a home run to Hank Aaron and his brother Tommie Aaron. I didn't realize there was going to be that much excitement at the game that day. I knew there was going to be some excitement because it was opening day and that Hank Aaron was closing in on the home run record but never did I imagine it was going to be that much. I remember Sparky (Anderson) my manager named me starting pitcher on that 4–4–1974 date. I was certainly very aware of the record and it did occur to me that he could hit it off of me on that day. I was no stranger to giving up home runs to Hank in the past. I know he tagged me for several over my career with him. I just didn't realize he was actually going to do it so quickly on that day. I always considered Hank as one of the best hitters out there so I shouldn't have been that surprised. But anyway, I faced Hank for 10 years in the National League and he hit 755 home runs over his career, so I guess giving up seven or eight home runs [to] him wasn't that bad! Again, there was so much excitement that day at the ballpark almost to the point of it being like a World Series atmosphere given all of the media and press covering the game. I remember Vice President Gerald Ford came through the clubhouse shaking everyone's hand. The atmosphere again was unbelievable, but then again not every day does someone like Hank Aaron come to the ballpark looking to hit home run number 714. It really was a great moment in our country's history and for baseball. Hank hit home run number 714 off of me on his first plate appearance with me. I remember I had a 3–1 count on him and the crowd started to boo because they thought I was going to walk him. But, the vast majority of the 50,000 fans in the stadium knew the pitch I had to throw him was . . . a fastball. And, I knew I had to throw him a fastball because I didn't want to walk him. And certainly, Hank Aaron knew what pitch I was going to throw him as well. The advantage always goes to Aaron when he knew what pitch was coming his way. I was hoping to throw the fastball down and away and hoped that he'd chase it, but the ball came a little over the plate and he didn't miss it. That ball didn't take that long to get out of the ballpark. For that split moment I thought it was going to hit the left field wall because it was a line drive, but it didn't and it went out for the home run. It never troubled me that Hank hit the home run off of me. I was just glad to be a part of history. Even though Hank did hit the home run off of me that day it wasn't that bad for us. We went on to win the game once the Big Red Machine got going.

"Hank was always one of those players that deserved respect. Whenever he hit a home run he never flipped the bat or pounded his fist. Hank would just hit the ball, run around the bases, and then go into the dugout. Hank is just a class act. Every day he was just the same. He never was this 'rah rah' kind of player. And, what most people don't realize, that game on April 4, 1974, almost didn't happen. The day before tornadoes hit in and around the Cincinnati area. I was a Florida kid and this was my first experience with one of those. So, there was a lot of concern because of the weather.

"I also remember I faced Hank a few innings later in that same game. I threw him another fastball and he did hit it hard but not hard enough. The crowd went crazy when he hit it thinking they were going to be a part of even more history, but they ended up being a part of just a little bit of history. He waited until he got to Atlanta for their opening day to break that record. So, for that moment there was a chance there wasn't going to be an Al Downing! But again, I was really proud to give up 714 and to be a part of this very important day in history."

—Jack Billingham (Major League pitcher 1968–1980 played for the Los Angeles Dodgers, Houston Astros, Cincinnati Reds, Detroit Tigers, and Boston Red Sox.)

Courtesy of the National Baseball Hall of Fame and Museum

"There was definitely a different feeling at the stadium that day on April 8, 1974. We were playing against a guy (Hank Aaron) who was on the verge of breaking Babe Ruth's all-time home run record. And, we as a team were all excited about it. It was all about Hank and we knew we were playing three games against the Braves and we were all hoping Henry would hit the home run to break the record against us and to be a part of this moment in baseball history. Fortunately for us, Henry accommodated our request. It was the most historic game I was ever a part of as a player and I was proud to be there.

"Henry's baseball career speaks for itself. Not many players in baseball history can fit in the same category and match the numbers Henry put up. He was such a terrific player and an equally terrific person. He handled the limelight as well as anyone. I'm sure it wasn't easy for him at the time. But what he did on that day in April was an incredible feat and we were so thrilled to be a part of it. In fact, the following week the Braves came to Dodgers Stadium and I was able to take two posters of that record-setting night and two baseballs over to the Braves clubhouse and I walked right up to Henry's locker and said, 'I didn't have the opportunity to ask you last week, but can I get your autograph?' and Henry graciously signed the items. I still have those posters and I still have those two signed balls from one terrific guy. Well, Henry deserves all of the accolades. He was chasing probably the greatest player in baseball history, Babe Ruth, and a record which he held so long, but Henry really ended up being the right guy to break that incredible record."

—Ron Cey (Major League third baseman, outfielder, and designated hitter 1971–1987; played for the Los Angeles Dodgers, Chicago Cubs, and Oakland Athletics.)

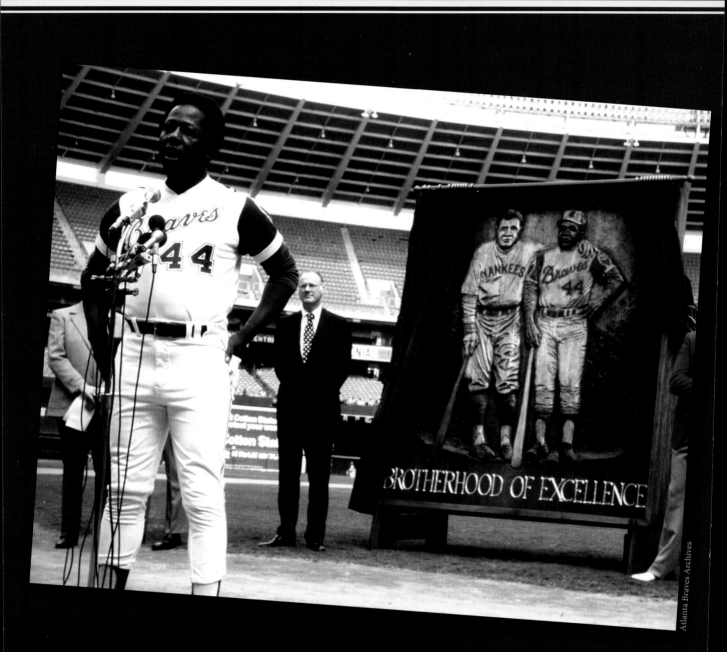

BROTHERHOOD OF EXCELLENCE

"As we look back at the prism of time events have a tendency to change, but it really was a busy time for us and Braves fans back on that April 8, 1974 day. Here is how it all started. My friend Britt Gaston and I, like so many others, wanted to be a part of this moment in history and see Hank Aaron hit this record-breaking home run. We were both baseball fans; Britt was probably more of a fan over the years than I was. But, I will always be a Hank Aaron fan! So, we went to the game with a small group of friends hoping to have a good time but being young guys you often find yourself mouthing off with one another and messing around. One thing led to another and Britt and I started to brag about knowing Hank Aaron and being friends with him. And then we said, 'We'll go and prove it!' Then I remember this one guy in particular egging us on. So, we said, 'Fine' and off we went. We gave our binoculars and stuff to the other guys and we were off. We marched our butts down to the lower seats. Then I think we said to ourselves once we got there, 'Now what?' I remember we squatted down and then when Hank Aaron came up in the bottom of the fourth inning and as soon as he hit the ball we jumped over the fence and onto the field. I don't even think the ball had cleared the wall for a home run yet. That would have been really awkward if the ball didn't go over and it was caught or it hit off the wall. Honestly, we were thinking with a seventeen-year-old brain and that wasn't bragging. We do remember thinking to ourselves how surprised we were there wasn't more commotion on the field or others jumping out there. I do remember there were two other guys who jumped the fence in the outfield, but they were quickly carted off being as drunk as they were. But, Britt and

I were clear-headed and I remember we just ran and ran and that was it. For the moment, it felt like the right thing to do, but the next morning we said, 'Oh, crap! What did we do?' It wasn't as cool the next day as it had been the night before. It was never intended to be this selfish act of us horning in on someone else's accomplishment, but rather it was just stupidity. We were just caught up in the moment and we wanted to congratulate this amazing man and this amazing accomplishment. But, it is what it is.

"And Hank Aaron has always been so gracious and kind to us over the years. Over the years, this moment has always followed us. Hank has always thought of our gesture as something two young guys just did because they were caught up in the moment. Hank is always the gentleman whenever asked. I have always viewed Hank Aaron as a person of integrity and who has carried himself well. To do what he did and under the circumstances he did them is something that I don't believe can happen again. I think he is a person of substance and that is always admirable even if you don't post the accomplishments as Hank did. Hank could have treated us in a number of ways and been justified in doing so, but he has been nothing but cordial and kind to us over the years. Britt and I were up in Atlanta a few years back and we were even invited to sign a few baseballs for Hank and his foundation. We were so happy to do so and to help out in any way we could.

"Unfortunately, Britt passed away in September, 2011, and over the years we had become close again like when we were younger. I remember we would have these chats and we would talk about those days fondly. It is amazing how this has continued to follow us around all of these years. I'm often asked did we get in trouble for what we did. The answer is yes we did! We both got locked up in jail for the night in the Atlanta downtown lock-up facility, which I don't recommend. The two of us got bailed out by Britt's father about 3:00 in the morning and needless to say he wasn't all too happy. I remember we went to court the next day and the judge said to the two of us if we were good boys for six months and we promised not to do anything like this again then this would all go away. We promised to do that and it did. I'll leave you with one quote by Britt he would say often over the years, knowing the security and the heightened sense that prevailed at the stadium on that day, he said, 'We would like to thank the bodyguards for their excellent judgment!' and Hank has always gotten a kick out of it."

—Dr. Cliff Courtney (Today he is an optometrist from Georgia, but back in 1974 he was an eager seventeen-year-old who ran onto the field when Henry Aaron broke Babe Ruth's home run record.)

"Willie Mays, Willie McCovey, Orlando Cepeda, Roberto Clemente, and Hank Aaron were just a few of the players who led by example. They went out there and played hard every day. You never saw them arguing with an umpire to get a call turned their way. They didn't complain if they were hurt. They just played. Hank Aaron epitomized that, he was so easygoing but when he did get mad he would just hit the ball harder the next time. He lived in an era that was quite different from the way we look and experience baseball today. Even the media was different then. They were not as obtrusive. Their job was just to report on the game or on baseball. Now, the media thinks they have to anoint the next member of the Hall of Fame or after a week they are predicting who will be in this year's World Series. And, because the world was so different Hank also never got the favorable press he should have over the years. It seemed like the media woke up in April, 1974, and said, 'Hey! Let's pay attention now to this guy.' no one was paying attention to this little team in Atlanta, especially when they are in a division which included the Dodgers and the Reds. They were the teams getting all of the press. But I remember the day quite vividly. The day wasn't about the two teams that were on the field that day, the Dodgers and the Braves. It was about a person and that person was Hank Aaron. I always wondered if anything would have changed regarding the press and their perception of Hank Aaron if he had played in New York or Los Angeles. Would he have been under any more scrutiny or would he have gotten the number of threats that he did get if he played somewhere else? All I ever knew for sure was that on that April 8, 1974 day it wasn't about me or my moment. I was just the pitcher who happened to give up the home run. That day was certainly all about Hank. People over the years have said to me, 'Don't you think you deserve more attention?' My reply back to them has always been, 'This was and will always be Mr. Aaron's moment. He was the only one there for all 715 home runs.' It's funny when you hear things like, 'You know, Hank Aaron never hit more than 50 home runs in a single season!' Then I think to myself, 'What does that have to do with anything?' It just seems to me that it is their way to somehow diminish Hank's record or career.

"Again, I was just the pitcher who happened to be on the mound that day. I remember during the 10th anniversary press event in Atlanta, which we were all there, back in 1984, some reporter asked Hank if that was the first home run he had ever hit off of me. Then Hank turned to me and said kiddingly, 'So Al, how many home runs did I hit off of you?' He said it kiddingly because he knew the answer was three. Hank could probably recall the game he hit them, what the temperature at game time was, and how far he hit them. Hank was amazing like that. I was just fortunate to be there and to be a part of some great moment in history. I never want to be in a situation to take any of the spotlight away from Mr. Aaron. You have to understand, Hank was a hero to so many of us as we made ourselves into this game. He was this beacon of light to us. I remember the pitch I threw Hank Aaron for the home run. It was a fastball inside, but it didn't matter what pitch you threw him. Hank was one of those unique ballplayers who basically looked for a pitch in a particular location and when it was in that spot he was generally going to hammer it. I guess that is why they called him 'Hammerin' Hank.' Hank was extremely patient; if he didn't get the pitch he was looking [for] then he would wait. The pitch I threw him again was a fastball that was supposed to come in on him, somewhat like a cut fastball, but it didn't. And Hank, like all of the great home run hitters, made you pay for your mistake. That is also why the good home run hitters hit a lot of home runs off of really good pitchers. Once Hank hit the pitch I had a pretty good idea the ball was leaving the ballpark. But, I also remembered that Hank would sometimes hit a lot of his balls with lots of topspin on it. So, for a moment I thought the ball might hit the top of the wall . . . but that wasn't the case that day. It was a line drive that left the ballpark very quickly. Hank didn't miss it. I remember I followed and watched the ball leave the ballpark. And for the majority of fans there was no doubt in their mind that the ball was going to be home run 715.

"I always found it interesting, and what most people don't remember is that there were several rain delays leading up to the game and there was some concern if the bad weather would return. So, I know they wanted to make the game official. Can you imagine if it would have been rained out before it became official and after Hank's home run? We would have to do this all over again. But, fortunately, the rain held out and it was a game for all to remember and I certainly will never forget it. I am so glad Mr. Aaron is being remembered more and more fondly as the years pass. The point is Hank Aaron hit 755 home runs and he was the individual who broke

Babe Ruth's record. Anyone who comes along afterwards would then have to break Hank Aaron's record. If you were fortunate enough to play against Hank Aaron as many years as I did you will never forget him. I was just so glad to compete against some of the greatest players who ever played this game and Hank is certainly at the top of that list."

—Al Downing (Major League pitcher 1961–1977; played for the New York Yankees, Oakland Athletics, Milwaukee Brewers, and Los Angeles Dodgers.)

"I look back to that April 1974 day fondly. I was on base when Henry hit home run number 715. I remember I ran around the bases so fast so this way I could clear home plate as quickly as possible and then make room for Hank. So many of us were just young ballplayers, and we were not just fellow teammates of Hank Aaron but we were also fans. When Hank broke the record for home runs it was at that time, and probably even today, one of the greatest moments in sports. I almost feel like Hank Aaron was chosen by a higher authority to do what he did. I don't think too many others could have done what he did. Hank was more than a superstar. We all learned so much from him. I remember Hank was so great to the younger ballplayers. He was so open to help us young kids. That made it so much easier for many of us. I was only twenty years old when I started to play for the Braves and he was always one of my idols. As a ballplayer you hope that your first experience in a major league clubhouse will be a positive one, and with Hank Aaron there it was. Hank wasn't flashy. He was just so good at doing what he did. Honestly, I can't remember him ever making a mistake. He was the best base runner I'd ever seen and he was such a great hitter besides all of those home runs. And, so many fans forget about that aspect of Hank's game. He was so well-rounded and I think that is what Hank wants to be remembered for. I think as he got closer to the home run record he became more of Hank Aaron the home run hitter. I remember he used to say, 'I'm not here to replace Babe Ruth. I'm just here to break his record.' And Hank well knows records are meant to be broken. Even if someone ever did break Hank's home run record they certainly would not have to go through what he went through. I mean Babe Ruth didn't go through it. Hank had to go through all of the scrutiny. Hank was a great leader and a great player. If you had to pick someone to emulate and how to play this game correctly it would be Hank Aaron. But even with all that I don't think he still gets the praise that he deserves. Over the years, you hear all of the debates regarding who is the best player of all time and I find it amazing how often Henry is left off the list. Given that, it is mind-boggling to think about his production as a player year in and year out. Hank was like magic. You could count on him all of the time. We used to call him 'Sup,' short for Superman or Superstar. I used to hit in front of him a lot and Dusty Baker used to hit behind him and the two of us used to be in awe of his ability and every once in a while we'd say to ourselves, 'How did he do that?' Hank was an amazing ballplayer. He deserves to receive all of the accolades and honors he is entitled to. I remember I was at a baseball Fantasy Camp a few years back with Bob Gibson and we were talking baseball. And I have always been one to ask questions. So, Bob and I were talking about players he faced during his brilliant career. I also like Bob because I hit my first home run off of him. I asked Bob who was the best he ever faced? I figured I'd ask one of the best pitchers of all time the question while I had him there. And then Bob looked at me like I was stupid and then he said, 'Don't you know?' and then Bob said, 'Willie (Mays), I could pitch him in and then he'd give up the outside corner of the plate and then I could get him out, and then I faced Mr. Aaron [and] none of that worked.' It was clear to me who he was saying was the best, especially when he said 'Mr. Aaron' and that it wasn't even close. Hank also made it easy for us when Davey and I hit 40 home runs each in 1973. I remember he took us both to the press conference they had about this feat and Henry told the media how proud he was of us and that meant the world to both of us. Hank had such a focus on the game and he wanted us all to be the best players we could be. Henry was always the guy who had your back as a teammate."

—Darrell Evans (Major League third baseman and first baseman 1969–1989 played for the Atlanta Braves, San Francisco Giants, and Detroit Tigers.)

"You are talking to the wrong man if you ever want me to talk about anything negative when it comes to Henry Aaron. If there was a better baseball player than Hank Aaron then I don't think he has been born yet. Henry was as perfect a ballplayer as they come. Hank was not a glory kind of guy. He was never a show boater. He never looked for the spotlight and nothing like that. Hank just played the game hard every day and did his job. Henry was such a team player. So, when it came to the home run record it was in reality just another game to Hank. Henry told us the day he broke Babe Ruth's record, 'I don't want to linger any longer with this record. So, I'm going to get it done early.' And, that he did. He never talked about the threats or the threatening letters he was receiving because he didn't want to place any pressure on us as teammates. You would have never known it but some of us, like Dusty (Baker) and I knew it. He would say to us that he wanted to get the record over with and put it behind him. He'd say, 'Let's get this behind us and concentrate on winning ballgames.' Henry is such a wonderful person to know. I never understood how you could have a problem with Henry because he was so nice and caring to everyone. Later on in his career, Henry would talk much more than he did early on in his career. He was constantly giving advice to me and Dusty. Hank was so amazing. No one remembers that he had 3600 hits during his career and that is unbelievable! Henry could do everything. He could hit for high percentage, he was a great base runner, he could field extremely well, and he would make very little mistakes. Henry stayed on the field. Meaning, he didn't get hurt a lot and when he did get hurt he played with the pain. Hank would tell us to play through the pain. He told that to Dusty and me because as Henry would put it, 'If you stayed in the game then no one can take your place in the field.' He would say, 'You can't help your club if you stay in the tub. So, stay healthy.' You would never see Hank in the Trainer's Room and yet you would see some guys in there all of the time. I tell people you really had to watch Henry play every day to really appreciate the type of ballplayer he was. To watch him do what he did you won't find a better player. You also couldn't find a better hitter, a base runner, a home run hitter, a better RBI guy, or an over-all better player. All Henry ever did was just get the job done. And, I'm not lying when it comes to the statements I am making. Henry Aaron was just amazing to me. He did everything one could do or expect from a teammate. He was this incredible leader by example. It makes me so proud to talk with Henry whenever we do. He is so educated and smart in a worldly way these days and he's such a great success. He seems to want to help everyone he meets. We had such a great time together and we continue to be great friends.

"There is one story I always like to share. One day Dusty and I came into the clubhouse and we were really tired, a day game after a night game. We were looking for something to help pep us up and get

HANK AARON

**hank aaron**

NEW ALL-TIME HOME RUN KING

OUTFIELD • ATLANTA BRAVES

HANK **AARON**

ATLANTA BRAVES

1st BASE

us going. I remember Hank called Dusty over, and he was a pretty good practical joker at times, and he gave him this tablet and he told him that it was a vitamin. Henry said, 'Take this, it will help.' So, Dusty did but what was so funny is that the tablet would turn your urine red. Hank knew it, but he liked to play a joke on us every once in a while. Shortly after Dusty took the tablet he went to the bathroom. The next thing I knew he was screaming for me and Henry to come in the bathroom. He said, "I'm about to die because my pee is red!" It scared Dusty to death. Henry and I never laughed so hard in our life. I guess I'll never understand it and it has certainly always confused me. I can never figure it out, why people didn't like Henry. What did he ever do? Some people hated him just because he played baseball. Not because of what he did to anybody."

—Ralph Garr (Major League outfielder 1968–1980 played for the Atlanta Braves, and Chicago White Sox, and California Angels.)

"The excitement was building up for almost a year. Late during the 1973 season Hank had the chance to break the record so the real hype began then. There was some off-season stuff, some good and some bad. There was all the controversy, including the hate mail and the death threats. But there was also a lot of really good things that came out of that off-season as well. I remember it was a really fun spring training in 1974. I myself was fortunate to make the ballclub. I was a low-end guy, or in other words I was the 10th man on a nine-man pitching staff. I was thrilled to be there and even more thrilled to make the club. We opened the season in Cincinnati and Hank hit a home run on opening day against Jack Billingham. And that home run tied him with Babe Ruth. Then the question was if Hank was going to play those final two games on Saturday and Sunday in Cincinnati or wait to go for the record at home. Then the Commissioner of Baseball got involved with the owner of the Braves ball club and mentioned something like it wouldn't look good if Hank sat out. I can't see Sparky Anderson and the Reds being that upset if they didn't have to face someone like Hank Aaron in the lineup.

"Traditionally, we probably should have had ten to fifteen thousand die-hard fans there for the game because we really weren't that good a ball club. But on that night, April 8, 1974, the stadium was packed and it was crazy with excitement. It was a sell-out crowd. It was one of those nights you didn't hear the noise but you felt it. Those on the team were very excited. I remember Sammy Davis Jr. came through the clubhouse before the game. I also remember how he said, 'If anyone catches the ball in the bullpen and is willing to give it up then I will give them

$25,000 for the ball.' That was a lot of money back then but those of us in the bullpen that night already decided during spring training that we would divide up the area in the bullpen, which was directly behind the left field wall. So each of us—me, Jack Aker, and Buzz Capra—divided up the area. Jack Aker, who had the most seniority, chose the area closest to the left field foul line because he was expecting Hank to pull the ball. I had the second-most seniority, so I positioned myself more towards left-center and Buzz was closer to center. So, when Hank came up in the first we all got into our positions and our territories. And after he didn't hit a home run then we took a seat. Then we got up again in the bottom of the fourth and I could see Al Downing throwing Hank a fastball and the next thing I remembered was that the ball was heading our way. I then said to myself, 'Hey! Wait that ball is coming to me!' I still remember like it as yesterday. Everyone talked about it being a great catch but if you pay attention to the video of the game you would have realized that if I didn't catch the ball then it would have hit me directly in the head. It was a really cool moment for me. I caught the ball . . . *[the]* ball! The next thing I remember after catching the ball was running to home plate and giving the ball to Henry while he was being hugged by his mother. There were tears in Henry's eyes. It was one of those moments in life you will never forget. I'm pretty sure Henry didn't know who I really was. I gave him the ball and said, 'Here you go Hammer!' And he said, 'Thanks kid!' I think in the excitement of the moment and with everything going on, there wasn't instant recognition but even to this day Henry calls me 'Tommy.' Henry and my mom are the only two people in my life who call me 'Tommy' and that is fine with me.  But, I think by then he was in a different place, an off-the-charts surreal moment for him. The real lifesaver moment was watching how his mother was hugging him. I think she was holding on to him so tightly because she was afraid he was going to get harmed. I had heard she was afraid Henry was actually going to get shot and that is why she was holding him so tightly. I guess that is the story within the story. But it was such a positive night for the fans, the team, and for the people of Atlanta. Shortly after I presented the ball to Henry I was pushed out of that inner circle. The game eventually played on, but the funny thing I remember was the stadium quickly dropped back to our ten to fifteen thousand die-hard fans. After the game, sportswriters came through the clubhouse hoping to capture quotes. I remember one of those writers was George Plimpton, who wrote *Paper Lion*. I remember he asked me a series of questions. One of those quotes made it to the Hall of Fame in the Henry Aaron exhibit. The quote is accompanied by the picture of me giving the ball to Henry. So, I guess you can say I made it to Cooperstown. I didn't get there as a player, but I got there. The good news is that catch was the highlight of my career and the bad news was that catch was the highlight of my major league career. I know I was new to the game, but I always knew there was something different about that April night. I kind of think, that night was possibly the first night Major League Baseball ever faced that much hoopla and calamity. What impressed me the most was how Henry went about his job and he did it all with this quiet and confident demeanor. I knew through Hank's inner circle of friends how difficult a time it was for him. There was so much pressure on him. There was so much socially and professionally going on. It was a really interesting time for baseball, the nation, and for Henry Aaron. Also, it always impressed me how Henry was never this flashy player and amazingly I don't ever remember him making a mental mistake while I was his teammate. All players make mistakes, but Henry seemed flawless.

"Henry was such a complete ballplayer. He hit more balls hard than any other player I ever witnessed as a player or a coach. Henry consistently performed, good, bad, or indifferent. Every one of his years would be someone else's career year. In the clubhouse, Henry was the backbone of the team. He made real, real good look easy. You never realized how good he was until you looked at the box score the next day. I think Henry played this game because he had such tremendous passion for the game. Every day he went to the ballpark he was constantly good. Even his bad days as a player would be good days for others.

"Catching the ball that night was pretty cool, but what most people don't realize is that there was a lot at stake that night. One of the companies who was a sponsor for the Braves was offering $25,000 to any fan who caught the ball. That is why there were all of those fishing nets out in the outfield stands and not to mention there was this offer by Sammy Davis Jr. that night to us in the bullpen. Everyone made a big deal of it because I ran the ball in from the bullpen to Henry but anyone out there in the bullpen would have done the same thing. But, to my surprise Magnavox, who was also a sponsor, presented me with an entertainment system. And, I got about $1500 in the mail from fans who thought what I did was pretty cool. I remember I got a $5 bill here or a $10 bill there. It really gave me hope for humanity. I remember my wife and I lived in this small apartment with our two small children and that entertainment system was pretty cool. I made out just fine for those who were asking. I may not have gotten that big cash payoff, but what I got was just fine for me. Again, it was the highlight of my career. I think I'm also in this third grade reader and of course you'll always find me in every baseball trivia book!"

—Tom House (Major League pitcher and pitching coach 1971–1978; played for the Atlanta Braves, Boston Red Sox, and Seattle Mariners. Coached for the Texas Rangers from 1985–1992.)

"You have to understand Hank Aaron was arguably the greatest ballplayer that ever lived. Hank was a fantastic hitter and he could do pretty much whatever he wanted to do. I could tell you so many stories. I remember this one that involved a pitcher with the San Francisco Giants, John 'The Count' Montefusco. Apparently, Montefusco was upset because his next scheduled start was against the lowly Atlanta Braves. I remember Henry telling the manager Eddie Mathews that he couldn't wait to face him. And, we all knew when Henry said something like that he was going to do something spectacular. The first time Henry was up there were two runners on and Montefusco threw him his best pitch, but that didn't matter to Henry, he hit the ball right out of the ballpark. Then, I remember Henry saying, 'I hope that teaches that cocky kid a lesson.' But, it always seemed, whenever something was needed Henry stepped up and did it. I remember as the end of the 1973 season approached, they pretty much shut down Henry because he was getting close to the record. That same year, Darrell Evans and I had just hit our 40th home runs and Henry was sitting on 39 home runs at that time. And Darrell said to Henry, 'You know there aren't going to be many teams out there that would have three players with 40 or more home runs in a season!' So, Henry said back to Darrell, 'Then

I'll play!' So, no sooner did he say that and found himself back in the line-up Henry ended up hitting a home run in his first at bat to give him 40 home runs as well for the year. We all knew Henry was going to break the record. It was no question Henry was going to be the person and that he was the right person to break the record because he was such an outstanding ballplayer. He was also such a smart ballplayer. Even when he took batting practice it was fun to watch. Every ball he hit he hit well. Sometimes he would even swing and miss purposely to see where his timing was.

"I remember I asked him once, 'What do you look for in a pitch?' Henry said, 'I look for a breaking ball.' I said,

Courtesy of the National Baseball Hall of Fame and Museum

'Really. You look for a breaking ball.' And Henry replied, 'Yeah, because I know they can't throw a fastball by me.' I then said, 'Yep. You got that right.' I'll say it and I'll say it again; Henry Aaron was an amazing ballplayer.

"I remember I used to have the locker right next to him and I think the only time I ever saw him get mad was when I changed the channel on his radio and he got all over me because he had these certain stations he listened to. He also knew it was me who changed the channel. I would have loved to be able to coach a Hank Aaron if I was a manager then. Henry was one of those ballplayers that carried ball clubs. As a manager, you always model your team after your best player. Henry would have been my best player. He led by example, whether he ran the bases, or was in the field, and of course at bat. Henry was the leader of the team and we all played in his shadow. He was just this tremendous talent and on the day he faced Al Downing and the Dodgers on April 8, 1974, we all knew what was going to happen. I remember a year or so later I was playing in Japan for the Yomiuri Giants and I was hitting in the same lineup, sixth, behind Sadaharu Oh when he broke Babe Ruth's home run record as well for Japanese Baseball. It's my favorite baseball trivia question."

—Davey Johnson (Major League second baseman and World Series Manager 1965–1978 who played for the Baltimore Orioles, Atlanta Braves, Yomiuri Giants, Philadelphia Phillies, and Chicago Cubs. Managed from 1984–2013 for the New York Mets, Cincinnati Reds, Baltimore Orioles, Los Angeles Dodgers, and Washington Nationals.)

"I remember the day Hank Aaron broke the record, but I couldn't think too much about the record or Hank because I had my own problems to worry about that night because I was the starting pitcher. I had my head pretty well wrapped up with my assignment of pitching against the Dodgers. I spent my time before the game with my pitching coach and my catcher talking about who was hitting well for the opposing team and who was swinging a good bat and how we should approach them from a pitching standpoint. However, we all knew there was something different about the game. We could feel it. What I noticed immediately was that Hank had a few bodyguards with him. Many of us knew he was receiving so much hate mail and threats. A lot of that started in the winter months leading up to the start of the 1974 season. Hank had ended the previous season with 713 home runs. So, I guess that gave a lot of idiots out there time enough to craft those letters of hate. I guess they didn't like the fact that this black man from the south was about to break this iconic record by a white ballplayer. I guess so many just couldn't handle it. I do know Hank had a lot on his mind and he had so much pressure. I know the Braves management wanted to sit out Hank that Saturday and Sunday in Cincinnati after he hit home run number 714 on opening day off of Jack Billingham. But the Commissioner of Baseball, Bowie Kuhn, ordered the Braves to play Hank because as he said, 'The people of Cincinnati paid to see Hank Aaron play.' But, Hank didn't care where he hit it, he just wanted to get it over with. After the winter months that passed and all of the pressure building up Hank Aaron being the ultimate professional he just wanted to get the job done and to put it behind him and get the record in the rearview mirror. Fortunately for the fans of Atlanta, he didn't hit the home run on Saturday or Sunday in Cincinnati.

"I remember I always had a lot of trouble facing the Dodgers over my career. And, I was pitching against Al Downing who was an excellent pitcher. I was very focused on my pitching assignment and it never occurred to me that I had the opportunity to be the winning pitcher on the night when Hank Aaron could break the record for home runs. That never really entered my mind. I was more worried about facing Garvey and Buckner and Cey than whether Henry was going to hit a home run. But, it really was all about Henry that night. We all knew it was his time. For me, I was grateful for Hank's home run because we were still trying to win a ball game and we had been behind 3–1 prior to Henry's home run. His home run made the score tied at 3–3 and shortly after that hit we went up by the score of 4–3. We eventually tacked on a few more runs and we ultimately won the game. And then, after the fact, I realized I got the victory on the day Hank Aaron broke the record and that was pretty cool in my book to be a part of that moment in baseball history. We recently had our 40th reunion in Atlanta in April 2014. I ran into Al Downing early in the day and we had the opportunity to sit down and chat about that night. I kidded him when I said, 'That he was remembered for giving up a home run.' That isn't always the best way to be remembered, but it didn't matter. 'I was trying to get him out,' Al told me. 'Hank got the best of me and it is a fact of life I've always had to live with,' he went on to say. I'm actually a little jealous of Al because I never gave up a famous home run during my pitching days. I did give up the first home run in the third deck at the old Braves Fulton

County Stadium. That is about it. It was way up there. I would say it pretty much equaled a $12 cab ride up there. As far as being a teammate with Hank, I spent six years with him in the Braves organization. Hank to me was always quiet, almost to the point of being shy. Hank never wanted the brass band or the red carpet. When Hank was in the clubhouse he was just one of the guys, he could kid with the best of them, and joke around. Hank was just a great, great teammate. I am so glad I never had to pitch against him! I was happier to have him as a teammate rather than an opponent."

—Ron Reed (Major League pitcher 1966–1984 played for the Atlanta Braves, St. Louis Cardinals, Philadelphia Phillies, and Chicago White Sox.)

"I had the opportunity to play against Hank Aaron when he hit home run number 714 against Jack Billingham on Opening Day in Cincinnati. I was playing left field at the time and I remember watching the ball leave the park as it was going over my head. But I go way back with Hank and I know he went through so much during his career and leading up to the record-breaking home run. I also know Hank wanted to hit that record-breaking home run in front of the hometown fans in Atlanta and I think he might not have wanted to play those final two games in Cincinnati but the Commissioner's Office insisted that he did play. The thing that impressed me the most about Henry really began for me during my first All-Star Game. Players like Willie Mays and Hank Aaron made us young players, many of who just recently came up to the big leagues, feel like we were a part of the team and welcomed us, and for that I will always be grateful and I will never forget it. These guys never had a chip on their shoulder or thought they were so much better than you. They just always made us feel like we were welcomed and that is why we as a team in the National League went on to win so many All-Star Games together. (From 1963 until 1982 the National League only lost one game to the American League.) Another reason is we took the game seriously and we had veteran players like Hank Aaron to help guide us. I remember I used to enjoy being around the batting cage during the All-Star Games because you would always find Hank there talking about hitting.

"It's funny, when I played I never knew about all of the bullshit Henry was experiencing at the time when he was approaching the home run record. All the hate mail and the threats he kept private. You would never know all of this was happening based on Henry's demeanor. He never let on to his team this was happening and that says a lot about how strong his character and personality was.

"I remember the day Henry hit home run number 715 like it was yesterday. I remember we had just played a day game against the Giants and I was on my way home to the hotel. I remember I ordered room service and I sat and watched the game. It was one of those moments of the game when you remember actually what you were doing at the time. From a competitor standpoint I wish I could have coached someone like Hank Aaron primarily because he would be easy to coach. You would just have to put his name in the lineup, third or fourth, and you didn't have to worry about him being late or missing batting practice, or infield practice because he would have been there day in and day out. Being a manager you wish every player could be like Hank Aaron. On a personal note, I do miss the game I love so much, and I miss just being around the ballpark.

"Henry was one of the fiercest competitors I faced in all of my years. Hank played defense and ran the bases and he was like poetry in motion. But, when he was a hitter he would grind it out. You had to get out Henry Aaron because he wasn't going to be in a situation to get himself out. Henry was a competitor like me, but I showed it differently. I was always in motion, diving into bases. Henry was aggressive but in a Hank Aaron kind of way. You don't put up the numbers and the stats like Henry did without being aggressive but he did it with dignity and grace. Henry Aaron was flawless. And, I know I made mistakes, I know I did, but my hope is that someday the powers to be will reconsider and give me a second chance, I won't need a third, but until then I will continue to support this game as much as I can and to continue to speak positively about it because I will never say anything negatively or bad-mouth something that I still love so much."

—Pete Rose (Major League infielder, outfielder, and manager 1963–1989 played for the Cincinnati Reds, Philadelphia Phillies, and Montreal Expos)

# Current Class

"Any player that was of that color during that era was of tremendous character, and then to dominate a sport when you are a minority like Hank Aaron did is astonishing. Any time you can perform at that level like Hank Aaron did is again another credit to his character. It is so encouraging because it kind of highlights the little struggle I have on a day to day basis and how that is nothing compared to the challenges Hank Aaron had to overcome on a daily basis. Because of what he did and to have that type of impact he had in the game should be an inspiration to the younger generation and for all generations to come."

—Chris Archer (Major League pitcher Tampa Bay Rays)

"Hank Aaron was certainly before my time, but over the years I've seen all of the footage and I watched him hit many home runs over the years, especially the famous one that broke Babe Ruth's record. Hank Aaron was a great ballplayer and my one wish is that I could have seen him play and in his prime. For me, he was one of those players I wish I was around to play against, like Willie Mays and Jackie Robinson. Those players could do it all on the field. It's easy to watch the tapes and see them out there, but I wish I could turn back the clock and been there to see them live and how they went about their business and how they approached the game. I never got the opportunity to meet Hank Aaron and it remains one of my goals to do so before I leave this game."

—Michael Bourne (All-Star outfielder, two-time Gold Glove recipient. Played for Philadelphia Phillies, Houston Astros, Atlanta Braves, and Cleveland Indians)

"I would love to meet him and hopefully I will have a chance to meet him soon. Definitely to put up the numbers he did back then while all of the racial concerns were such a part of the game is unbelievable. Interestingly, I never saw him play, but I know everything about him by seeing so many of his highlights. He had such a sweet stroke and he had such great power. He probably could have hit backwards if he liked!"

—Domonic Brown (All-Star outfielder Philadelphia Phillies)

"Being a Hank Aaron Award winner and then meeting the man the award has been named after means a lot to me. I've won many awards during my career so far, but winning the Hank Aaron Award was one of the greatest moments for me in this game primarily because of the man behind the award. I was very proud to win the award and it also allowed me to meet Hank Aaron for the first time and that was a very special moment for me. I knew at that moment I was standing next to a legend."

—Miguel Cabrera (All-Star infielder, World Series Champion, two-time MVP award winner, Triple Crown winner, five-time Silver Slugger Award winner, three-time Batting Champion, two-time Home Run Champion, two-time RBI leader, and two-time recipient Hank Aaron Award winner. Played for Florida Marlins, Detroit Tigers)

"I've seen footage of Hank Aaron all of my life and you can tell he was one of the greatest players who has ever played this game. Hank Aaron was also such a great role model. Hank Aaron remains as a great example to us all that we too can achieve greatness as well and that no door will ever stop us as long as we continue to fight hard and to believe in ourselves."

—Chris Carter (Major League ballplayer
Oakland Athletics, Houston Astros)

Courtesy of The National Baseball Hall of Fame and Museum

"I had the opportunity to meet Hank Aaron on several occasions. Hank is really a great guy. Being a power hitter like I am, I am very thankful Hank Aaron came around. He was one of the first players to be remembered for that type of hitting and it only helped us who are also power hitters who came around over the years. What he did for the game by changing the game for power hitters is really special to me . . . but to be fair and not to understate his greatness, Hank Aaron was just a great all-around ballplayer."

—Prince Fielder (All-Star first baseball and MVP, three-time Silver Slugger Award winner, National League Homerun Champion, two-time Home Run Derby Champion, and recipient Hank Aaron Award winner. Played for Milwaukee Brewers, Detroit Tigers, Texas Rangers)

"I will always remember a few weeks before I signed with the Atlanta Braves they invited me down to Atlanta Stadium and I got to hit batting practice with Andruw Jones, Gary Sheffield, and Chipper Jones. It was like a dream and it was a pretty big deal for a kid that was only eighteen years old. And then they brought Hank Aaron out for me to meet. From that point on, the thing I remember the most about Hank Aaron is the presence he brings to any situation. There is always something special when Hank Aaron is there whether it's before a game, at a players banquet, or during spring training. I guess you kind of feel the same thing when the president of the United States enters a room. Yet, when you start talking to Hank you realize what a down-to-earth guy he really is. That is what most people don't realize despite all the negative things that happened from the racial component he faced to all of the demands the media places on him, but then he has time to talk to this eighteen-year-old kid. Growing up in the Atlanta area and being a Braves fan all of your life you immediately know the impact Hank Aaron has had on the game and for society in general. Even though I never saw Hank Aaron play the game you do have these memories and images of what he did for this game, and I believe that is what separates the great ones because there are the stories that are passed down from one generation to the next. For example, I feel like I know Hank Aaron because of the stories my dad told me and one day I'll pass them on to my own kids. That is also why I call him the Home Run King because that is what my father told me he was. And, I kind of feel like that is what most other baseball [players and fans] feel as well . . . that he is the undisputed Home Run King. It was a pleasure getting to know Hank Aaron and I know he will always be synonymous with the game and to all Braves fans."

—Jeff Francoeur (Major League outfielder and Gold Glove recipient. Played for Atlanta Braves, New York Mets, Texas Rangers, Kansas City Royals, San Francisco Giants, San Diego Padres)

"Hank Aaron is a trailblazer. Hank Aaron, along with players such as Jackie Robinson, Willie Mays, Satchel Paige, and Frank Robinson were just some of the players to help pave the way for many of us modern-day players. Without them, I might not be a pitcher in today's game. I remember watching the footage of Hank Aaron hitting the home run that broke Babe Ruth's record and knowing what impact that had on the game, and even though I was not around to personally witness the hit it will always be a part of my baseball memories."

—Sam Freeman

(Major League pitcher St. Louis Cardinals)

"Being a recipient of the Hank Aaron Award is a great honor. Winning any baseball award is pretty special, but the Hank Aaron Award is such a prestigious honor and I am so happy that I was able to represent the National League. Growing up I never had the opportunity to see Hank Aaron play, but I certainly heard about the stories of what a great player he was for baseball fans. To me, my greatest memory of watching all of the highlights that spans his career was when he

Courtesy of The National Baseball Hall of Fame and Museum

hit that 715th home run and becoming the all-time Home Run King as he ran around the bases. It is a clip that I have seen hundreds of times and from a fan's perspective that is why the home run is so important and that is why it is talked about so much. Hank Aaron is also a model of consistency. For him to do what he did year in and year out is a pretty special achievement for those of us who play the game because it is one of the hardest things to do . . . to be consistently good. This consistency helps define the greatest players of all time. Unfortunately, I have never officially met Hank Aaron and I am hoping that will change some day. I even played a year in Mobile, Alabama, Hank Aaron's hometown, and at a stadium named in his honor but I never crossed paths with him, but again I am hoping one day I will get the chance to meet him. All I want to do is to shake his hand. It would be awesome to meet him and maybe I can pick up a hitting tip or two!"

—Paul Goldschmidt (All-Star first baseman, Silver Slugger Award winner, three-time Batting Champion, Home Run Co-Leader, RBI leader, Gold Glove winner, and recipient Hank Aaron Award. Played for Arizona Diamondbacks)

"It is kind of ironic that even though I didn't ever see him play I have always been around players that did and who told me some great stories about Hank Aaron. I know he started to hit with his hands the wrong way and even though there is no film footage of that it's nice to keep those stories going. I know he wasn't physically the biggest player out there but people around me told me that he had the quickest hands in the game. Aaron had such great overall ability in this game, but everyone wanted to see him hit the long ball. As players you gotta know the history of this game and you gotta know what Hank Aaron meant to this game."

—Curtis Granderson (All-Star outfielder, Silver Slugger Award winner, and RBI leader. Played for Detroit Tigers, New York Yankees, New York Mets)

"My fondest memory of Hank Aaron was when he threw out the first pitch at the start of the 2010 baseball season. It was also my very first game in the major leagues and I got the opportunity to catch the ball thrown by Hank Aaron that day. It was a feeling, even today, that is hard to describe. It was almost surreal. My family and friends were there and everyone that was close to me was there for my first game, and then to have Hank Aaron there to share his support and wish me and my team well was so awesome. I remember Hank wished me well on opening day; he encouraged me to have a great season. He told me not to worry. He said, 'You'll be great,' and to 'Have fun!' I could tell he had so much confidence in me. I also had a chance to meet Hank Aaron in spring training leading up to the season. We sat down and we had a great conversation and it was there he told me 'If you have any questions then please come by my offices at the stadium,' and then he ended our meeting with the words 'You have my full support!' It was truly a special moment for me."

—Jason Heyward (All-Star outfielder and two-time Gold Glove winner. Played for Atlanta Braves; plays for St. Louis Cardinals)

"Hank Aaron definitely means a lot to me. Hank Aaron stands as one of the greatest African American players that has ever played this game and he played during a very difficult timeframe. He remains a great symbol and role model for all of us to look up to and admire. Even today, so many young people look up to Hank Aaron. If it wasn't for men like Hank Aaron I might not be playing this game today!"

—Aaron Hicks (Major League outfielder Minnesota Twins)

"To me, Hank Aaron was and forever will be one of the greatest players of all time. To do what he did for the number of years he did what he did is a tribute to his character. And, to surpass the great Babe Ruth with the all-time home run record, in all that adversity demonstrates what type of person he was. Hank Aaron was such a great ballplayer and you can even see it today how so many in baseball want to be like him and to emulate him both on and off the field. Hank Aaron is one of those guys I would like to thank because I wouldn't be here today without the sacrifices he and so many made."

—L. J. Hoes (Major League outfielder. Played for Baltimore Orioles, Houston Astros)

"Meeting Hank Aaron for the first time leaves you speechless. Knowing all that he has done for the game of baseball and then for me to win an award that has his name on it is one of the greatest honors a player of today can achieve, especially for me. Meeting Hank Aaron for the first time was a surreal experience. Primarily because, being a ballplayer in today's game the name Hank Aaron represents someone you've only heard about, and you know your parents were the ones who used to enjoy seeing him play, again, made the experience somewhat surreal for me because of what a legend Hank Aaron is. I remember when I won the Hank Aaron Award in 2006 he was there and then he handed me and Derek Jeter the plaque and then he shook our hands. I've received many awards in this game, the Rookie of the Year Award in 2005 and the Most Valuable Player Award in 2006, but to receive the Hank Aaron Award is one of the highlights of my career because Hank Aaron will always be a special person to me and such an important player in baseball history."

—Ryan Howard (All Star first baseman, World Series Champion, MVP (Most Valuable Player) Award winner, National League Rookie of the Year recipient, Silver Slugger Award winner, two-time Home Run Champion, three-time RBI leader, Home Run Derby Champion, and Hank Aaron Award winner. Played for Philadelphia Phillies)

"Hank Aaron has been a huge impact on my career. If it wasn't for Jackie Robinson then there wouldn't have been Hank Aaron. And, if it wasn't for Hank Aaron then there wouldn't have been Ernie Banks. And, if it wasn't for Ernie Banks then there wouldn't have been Reggie Jackson. And, if it wasn't for Reggie Jackson then there wouldn't have been Ken Griffey Jr. And, if it wasn't for Ken Griffey Jr. then there wouldn't have been Derek Jeter. And finally, if it wasn't for Derek Jeter then there wouldn't have been *me*! Hank Aaron did a lot of amazing and great things for this game and for an African American to break Babe Ruth's record is a monumental task and achievement. Hank Aaron transformed the game. Records were meant to be broken and that is why Hank Aaron is the Home Run King."

—Orlando Hudson (All-Star outfielder and four time Gold Glove recipient. Played for Toronto Blue Jays, Arizona Diamondbacks, Los Angeles Dodgers, Minnesota Twins, San Diego Padres, Chicago White Sox)

"I first met Hank Aaron at the 2002 All-Star Game in Milwaukee and I had the opportunity to shake his hand. I was only about twenty-five or twenty-six years old at the time and it was a very special moment in my baseball career. It was my first All-Star Game, my family and friends were all watching, and it had this huge national presence to the game. And then I robbed Barry Bonds of a home run in the game when I grabbed the ball over the wall. For me it was a lot of firsts for me that day. I lived every kid's dream all in one game. Looking back even to this day, it was one of the best highlights of my career. It really did feel like a dream. But back to Hank Aaron. I am a tremendous fan and I can't imagine what this man must have went through when he was about to set the home run record. All of the death threats, the pressure of breaking this iconic baseball record, the bodyguards around you and your family, and of course all of the death threats. Hank Aaron had so much going on and yet he endured and stayed strong and amazingly he was able to stay focused and concentrate on the game of baseball. You talk about a true professional; Hank Aaron was the epitome of a true professional. Hank Aaron was one of the first names I got to know and follow as I was growing up. Hank Aaron and Jackie Robinson are two names that you really have to stop and say to yourself 'Wow!' These guys are baseball, they are a part of history, and they are sheer greatness. I personally want to thank players such as this for what they did in this game because if they weren't successful then there is a chance then I might not be successful in this game. I may have been playing but I don't think I would be where I am without the obstacles men like this endured and the eventual success they achieved. I probably would have focused on football, but when you are young and hear about all of the stories concerning Jackie

Robinson, Hank Aaron, and Willie Mays it then helps you as an African American kid, who grew up in the inner city, to push along and try and make a name for myself. It gives you the motivation because if they can do it and face this adversity then you can do it too. I remember the first person I called after that first All-Star Game and my chance meeting with Hank Aaron was my granddad because he was the individual who first got me interested in baseball. My granddad's

name was George Cobbs and he played a little baseball in the Negro Leagues. He helped introduce me to the game and I remember how he used to sit down with me and he used to teach me all about the great names, Jackie Robinson, Hank Aaron, Satchel Paige, Cool Papa Bell, Ray Dandridge, and Josh Gibson. I remember when I told him that I got the chance to shake Hank Aaron's hand he said, 'Say, what! That is really cool!' My granddad lived his excitement through me because he never made it to the major leagues, but he helped put his dreams in me. So, when I made it to the big leagues it was a special moment for him too. It was my granddad who taught me these stories of the Negro Leagues and how each of these men endured and again paved the way for the generations to come."

—Torii Hunter (All-Star outfielder, two-time Silver Slugger Award winner, nine-time Gold Glove recipient. Played for Minnesota Twins, Los Angeles Angels of Anaheim, Detroit Tigers)

"All I can say [is] it was a tremendous record he achieved and yet in doing so he continued to help his team win ballgames. I know he faced so many obstacles and so much adversity and because he moved forward and kept swinging the bat it only shows the strong character of the man."

—Austin Jackson (Major League outfielder for the Detroit Tigers and Seattle Mariners)

"To do what Hank Aaron did during that timeframe, when there was such turmoil that was gripping the country at the time, could not have been easy for any man. It could not have been easy doing what Hank Aaron did based on the circumstances of the time, but this only highlights how strong his character and what type of man he is. Hank Aaron is and always will be a great role model for us all and someone to look up to."

—John Jay (Major League outfielder and World Series Champion for the St. Louis Cardinals)

"To me Hank Aaron is an icon! I have always felt like I have had this connection to him because the two of us are from the same state. Hank Aaron's name is one of the most recognized names out there and it is the most recognized name in the state of Alabama. For him to be able to represent the state and the city of Mobile is really awesome. He went through so much, playing as he did through all of that adversity and to suffer through all of those difficult situations and then to eventually overcome it is a credit to Mr. Aaron. Hank Aaron is someone I will always look up to."

—Desmond Jennings (Major League outfielder for Tampa Bay Rays)

Atlanta Braves Archives

"I met Hank Aaron on several occasions and he is always gracious and friendly. He symbolizes a lot to me as an African American more than I can ever explain. What he has done for this game of baseball is truly remarkable. What he has been able to accomplish given all of the adversity, all of the negativity, all of the pressure is simply amazing. It was Hank Aaron who helped us to realize that we can accomplish anything and that is what I try and do every day in this game."

—Adam Jones (All-Star outfielder, four-time Gold Glove recipient, and Silver Slugger Award winner. Played for Seattle Mariners and Baltimore Orioles)

"Hank Aaron was one of the best hitters of his generation. I admired his style of play and consistency throughout his career. His ability to go out and perform the way he did with the death threats because he was close to breaking Babe Ruth's record was something I will always admire. I've heard the stories of how hard-working and dedicated to his career he was. I've only read a few books and have seen highlights of Hank's baseball games but early on I knew he was the type of player that I wanted to model myself and my game after."

—Howie Kendrick (All-Star infielder for the Los Angeles Angels of Anaheim; plays for Los Angeles Dodgers)

"I have never had the honor of meeting Hank Aaron but I want to someday. Hank Aaron is one of those players that is on my bucket list to meet. Hank Aaron means a great deal to me. Hank Aaron is someone I have always looked up to when I was growing up. To me he will always be the Home Run King and I will always remember that image of him breaking the home run record and watching those two young guys running on the field. It is an image that will always stick with me forever. Hank Aaron never struck me as this flashy or flamboyant guy but when you look back at his career he certainly took care of business when he needed to!"

—John Mayberry Jr. (Major League outfielder/first baseman for the Philadelphia Phillies, Toronto Blue Jays, and New York Mets)

Atlanta Braves Archives

"There was a reason why they called him Hammerin' Hank. Hank wasn't a big guy, but despite all of that he could hit the ball very far. He had so much talent. Yet, despite all of that talent he had to overcome so much adversity during his playing days. It's funny, we as players today think we have it bad when the fans get on us or heckle us, but back in Hank Aaron's day it must have been a thousand times worse. We can learn a lot from Hank Aaron as players today knowing the pressure and adversity he faced and the strong mentality he had to overcome."

—Andrew McCutchen (All-Star outfielder, MVP (Most Valuable Player) Award winner, three-time Silver Slugger Award winner, and Gold Glove recipient. Played for the Pittsburgh Pirates)

"I remember the first time I met Hank Aaron, it was in the Bahamas. I was having breakfast at the hotel with my family when all of a sudden these two little children came up to me. They said, 'Mr. Ortiz, can we get your autograph?' I then turned around to see them and sign their autographs and who was standing next to them but Hank Aaron. It was his grandchildren and they were staying at the same resort. I was speechless. The only thing I could say was, 'I should be getting your autograph!' But then I won the Hank Aaron Award the next year and that made it even more special."

—David Ortiz (All-Star first baseman/designated hitter, World Series Champion, World Series MVP (Most Valuable Player), six-time Silver Slugger Award winner, seven-time Edgar Martinez Award winner, American League Home Run leader, two-time RBI leader. He holds the Major League record for Home Runs, RBI, and hits by a designated hitter. Played for the Minnesota Twins and Boston Red Sox)

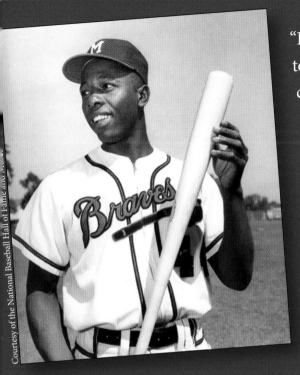

"Hank Aaron is one of those players that has helped to pave the way for all players and especially African American ballplayers. He began his career in the Negro Leagues and then eventually the major leagues and he was just so consistent year in and year out. Hank Aaron is a mark of consistency and so many think of him as just a home run hitter but because of that consistency he was so much more than that. Hank Aaron had nearly 3800 hits, all of those RBIs, the Gold Gloves he earned, and I honestly think a lot of this gets lost in the shuffle and the average fan doesn't realize how consistently good he was and how complete a ballplayer Hank Aaron was. He was one of the greatest ever to play this game. Even today, Hank Aaron remains as one of the greatest Ambassadors for this sport. Hank Aaron always did what was right for this game. I have a tremendous amount of respect for him and being from Mobile too I respect him even more. Hank Aaron did it the right way and got it done."

—Juan Pierre (Major League outfielder, World Series Champion, Roy Campanella Award winner, and the James "Cool Papa" Bell Legacy Award winner from the Negro Leagues Baseball Museum. Played for Colorado Rockies, Florida Marlins, Chicago Cubs, Los Angeles Dodgers, Chicago White Sox, Philadelphia Phillies, Miami Marlins)

"Hank Aaron is number one in the record books and that is pretty special for any category in baseball. He played this game for a very long time and he put up some incredible numbers. I know about him and he is a fun player to look back on and respect. Hank Aaron did it all and was a complete ballplayer. Hank Aaron suffered through so much and because of these sacrifices it allowed someone like me to be able to play this game today."

—David Price (All-Star pitcher, Cy Young Award winner, American League ERA and wins leader in 2012. Played for the Tampa Bay Rays and Detroit Tigers)

"Everyone has an opinion of Hank Aaron and being an Atlanta native you certainly know what he has done and what he has accomplished. Hank Aaron is a great man, he was great for the game, and he was a blessing for the game as well. He broke the home run record that they said couldn't be done and that makes him a one-of-a-kind person. As a fellow ballplayer you have to respect him because he came to the ballpark ready to play every day. As for me, who is not a home run kind of player, it is unbelievable to think of the numbers he put up in that category alone. He did what he did and he never was a show-boater or flashy. Hank Aaron played the game hard and he played it the right way."

—Ben Revere (Major League outfielder for the Minnesota Twins and Philadelphia Phillies)

Hank Aaron Museum in Mobile, Alabama

"Players like Jackie Robinson, Willie Mays, and Hank Aaron were just some of the players who helped set the stage so that the rest of us who play this game today . . . can. Fortunately, at the same time these players came into the game things in America started to change. I have always given tremendous credit to these players who had to go through the fire in years past so that players like me could get the chance and the opportunities we do. To me, Hank Aaron was one of the greatest players this game has ever seen and he is the undisputed Home Run King. No one has ever questioned what he did in this game, and no one questions his integrity, not to mention what he had to go through to eventually accomplish what he did."

—Jimmy Rollins (All-Star shortstop, World Series Champion, MVP (Most Valuable Player) Award winner, Silver Slugger Award winner, and four-time Gold Glove recipient. Played for Philadelphia Phillies; plays for Los Angeles Dodgers)

"Hank Aaron was a little before my time, but he is one of two players I wish I could have seen play; the other was Willie Mays. He did so much and was so good at what he did. The funny thing I heard about him was that he didn't ever swing the bat the right way when he first came up . . . he swung it cross-handed! That is amazing given what he was able to accomplish. He got through it all and stayed strong-minded to succeed. Especially, during a time, for him to do what he did was pretty amazing to me. I just wish I was old enough to see him play. I'm not sure enough of us appreciate what Hank Aaron did, but I do!"

—B. J. Upton (Major League outfielder for the Tampa Bay Devil Rays, Tampa Bay Rays, and Atlanta Braves)

"I finally got the opportunity to meet Hank Aaron the day I signed with the Atlanta Braves at my press conference in 2013. Hank Aaron is one of these iconic players that has done so much for this game, and so much for the town I now call home. He was this great symbol for the game. You only hear about the good things that are associated with him when you hear his name. What he has done for this game and what he has done for this community are two significant achievements he will always be remembered for. And, of course, what he has done on the field during his playing days is unbelievable. It is almost impossible to imagine what he must have went through and then to do what he did speaks volumes for the man and his character. It is always awesome to hear about his accomplishments even though I never got the opportunity to see him play. I will always remember the words he said to me during our first conversation, 'Welcome to the team, welcome to Atlanta, and most of all have fun.' Hank Aaron still knows this is a kid's game and for him to keep it that simple and make that type of statement meant the world to me."

—Justin Upton (All-Star outfielder and two-time Silver Slugger Award recipient. Played for Arizona Diamondbacks, Atlanta Braves; plays for San Diego Padres)

"Hank Aaron means a lot to me. He came into this game at a very difficult time for African American ballplayers. But, then he went on to break a record that meant a lot to baseball fans and then he achieved this quest for the record after facing all of that controversy. Hank Aaron must have been a great teammate because he played at the top of his game through all of these challenges and it never affected his play and as a result he continued to thrive."

 —Delmon Young (Major League outfielder and designated hitter. Played for the Tampa Bay Devil Rays, Minnesota Twins, Detroit Tigers, Philadelphia Phillies, Tampa Bay Rays, Baltimore Orioles)

# Hank Aaron Career Statistics

**Born:** February 5, 1934 in Mobile, Alabama

**Debut:** April 13, 1954 (Age 20)

**Teams:** Milwaukee Braves/Atlanta Braves/Milwaukee Brewers 1954–1976

**Final Game:** October 3, 1976 (Age 42)

| Year | Tm | AB | R | H | HR | RBI | SB | BB | SO | BA |
|------|-----|-----|-----|-----|-----|-----|-----|-----|-----|------|
| 1954 | MLN | 122 | 58 | 131 | 13 | 69 | 2 | 28 | 39 | .280 |
| 1955 | MLN | 153 | 105 | 189 | 27 | 106 | 3 | 49 | 61 | .314 |
| 1956 | MLN | 153 | 106 | 200 | 26 | 92 | 2 | 37 | 54 | .328 |
| 1957 | MLN | 151 | 118 | 198 | 44 | 132 | 1 | 57 | 58 | .322 |
| 1958 | MLN | 153 | 109 | 196 | 30 | 95 | 4 | 59 | 49 | .326 |
| 1959 | MLN | 154 | 116 | 223 | 39 | 123 | 8 | 51 | 54 | .355 |
| 1960 | MLN | 153 | 102 | 172 | 40 | 126 | 16 | 60 | 63 | .292 |
| 1961 | MLN | 155 | 115 | 197 | 34 | 120 | 21 | 56 | 64 | .327 |
| 1962 | MLN | 156 | 127 | 191 | 45 | 128 | 15 | 66 | 73 | .323 |

| Year | Tm | AB | R | H | HR | RBI | SB | BB | SO | BA |
|------|----|----|----|----|----|-----|----|----|----|----|
| 1963 | MLN | 161 | 121 | 201 | 44 | 130 | 31 | 78 | 94 | .319 |
| 1964 | MLN | 145 | 103 | 187 | 24 | 95 | 22 | 62 | 46 | .328 |
| 1965 | MLN | 150 | 109 | 181 | 32 | 89 | 24 | 60 | 81 | .318 |
| 1966 | ATL | 158 | 117 | 168 | 44 | 127 | 21 | 76 | 96 | .279 |
| 1967 | ATL | 155 | 113 | 184 | 39 | 109 | 17 | 63 | 97 | .307 |
| 1968 | ATL | 160 | 84 | 174 | 29 | 86 | 28 | 64 | 62 | .287 |
| 1969 | ATL | 147 | 100 | 164 | 44 | 97 | 9 | 87 | 47 | .300 |
| 1970 | ATL | 150 | 103 | 154 | 38 | 118 | 9 | 74 | 63 | .298 |
| 1971 | ATL | 139 | 95 | 162 | 47 | 118 | 1 | 71 | 58 | .327 |
| 1972 | ATL | 129 | 75 | 119 | 34 | 77 | 4 | 92 | 55 | .265 |
| 1973 | ATL | 120 | 84 | 118 | 40 | 96 | 1 | 68 | 51 | .301 |
| 1974 | ATL | 112 | 47 | 91 | 20 | 69 | 1 | 39 | 29 | .268 |
| 1975 | MIL | 137 | 45 | 109 | 12 | 60 | 0 | 70 | 51 | .234 |
| 1976 | MIL | 85 | 22 | 62 | 10 | 35 | 0 | 35 | 38 | .229 |
| 23 | | 3298 | 2174 | 3771 | 755 | 2297 | 240 | 1402 | 1383 | .305 |

*Statistics courtesy of Baseball-Reference.com